Development-Induced Displacements in Zimbabwe

Learning from Colonial
and
Post-Colonial Experiences

Development-Induced Displacements in Zimbabwe
Learning from Colonial
and
Post-Colonial Experiences

Edited by

Centre for Conflict Management and Transformation
& Tugwi Mukosi Multidisciplinary Research Institute

Published in 2021 by
Weaver Press, Box A1922 Avondale, Harare, Zimbabwe
<www.weaverpresszimbabwe.com>
and
Centre for Conflict Management and Transformation
28 Oxford Avenue, Newlands, Harare
P.O. Box A 1755, Avondale, Harare
Website: www.ccmt.co.zw

© Centre for Conflict Management and Transformation. 2021

Typeset by Weaver Press

The editors would like to express their gratitude to Weltfriedensdienst e.V. (WFD) and Ziviler Friedensdienst (ZFD) for supporting the publication of this book.

All rights reserved. No part of the publication may be reproduced, stored in a retrieval system or transmitted in any form by any means – electronic, mechanical, photocopying, recording, or otherwise – without the express written permission of the publisher.

DISCLAIMER: Any views or opinions presented or represented in this book are personal and belong solely to the authors and do not represent those of people, institutions, companies or organisations that the authors may or may not be associated with in personal or professional capacity. Any views or opinions are not intended to malign any group of people, institution, company, organisation, or individual.

ISBN: 978-1-77922-386-9 (p/b)
ISBN 978-1-77922-387-6 (ePub)
ISBN: 978-1-77922-388-3 (pdf)

Contents

About the Authors		vii
Foreword		
Amb. Mary S. Mubi		xi
Introduction		
Tugwi Mukosi Multidisciplinary Research Institute		xiv
Key Issues and Recommendations		
Centre for Conflict Management and Transformation		xxi

I. Perspectives on History, Law and Policy

1. Development-Induced Displacements in Zimbabwe: A Historical Overview and General Experiences of the Affected People
   Hon. Chief Ngungumbane — 3

2. Development, Land Acquisition and Displacement: An Analysis of the Extent of the Compliance by the Laws of Zimbabwe to the Kampala Convention
   Thammary Brenda Vhiriri — 18

3. Land Tenure Systems, Neoliberal Policies and Displacement in Zimbabwe: An Overview
   Steve Mberi — 39

II. Colonial Experiences

4. One Dam, Two Different Relocation Processes: The Case of Kariba, 1956-1961
   Terence M. Mashingaidze — 73

5. Colonial and Post-Colonial Relocation Experiences of Two Headmen in Zaka District
   Francis Muromo — 99

III. Post-Colonial Experiences

6. The Resettlement and Compensation of Displaced Households: A Case Study of Marovanyati and Causeway Dam Projects
   Chrispen Maseva — 111

7. Displacement Due to Urban Expansion in Mazowe
   District: Illustrations from Selected Urban Settlements
   Joel Chaeruka — *118*

8. Challenges to Relocation and Compensation of Rural
   Communities Displaced by Development Projects: Case
   Studies from the Midlands Province
   Christof Schmidt & Shadreck Vengesai — *137*

About the Authors

Centre for Conflict Management and Transformation (CCMT) is a non-governmental organisation based in Harare, Zimbabwe. CCMT works to transform the ways in which societies deal with conflict – away from adversarial approaches and towards collaborative problem solving.

Tugwi Mukosi Multidisciplinay Research Institute (TMMRI) is a research institution of the Midlands State University (MSU) integrating multi-disciplinary researches that address national development priorities in water, environment, agriculture, fisheries, energy, livelihoods, and rural development.

Ambassador Mary S. Mubi is a diplomat and senior public servant in the Government of Zimbabwe. In the early 1980s, she worked in community development and adult education, as the government mobilized local communities to participate in inclusive local government structures. During her long diplomatic career, she served as the country's representative in Rome to the Food and Agricultural Organization of the United Nations (FAO), the World Food Programme (WFP) and the International Fund for Agriculture (IFAD). Her current post in the Office of the President and Cabinet has cemented her commitment to the importance of robust governance structures that are able to mobilize communities and a multiplicity of actors and development partners in the achievement of inclusive socio-economic development.

Honourable Chief Ngungumbane is a traditional Chief in Mberengwa (since 2006), member of the Chiefs Council (since 2008), Provincial Chairperson for the Midlands Provincial Assembly of Chiefs (since 2008) and Senator representing Chiefs of the Midlands Province in the upper chamber of the Zimbabwean Parliament (since 2008). He holds an MSc in Peace, Leadership & Conflict Resolution and a BSc (Hons) in Psychology with the Zimbabwe Open University.

Thammary Brenda Vhiriri is a legal practitioner with an LLBS from the University of Zimbabwe, Masters in Public Administration from Women's University in Africa, and concluding an LLM in Corporate Law with the University of South Africa. She has worked with the Public Service Commission, Ministry of Mines and Mining Development, African Diamond Producers Association, and was a government legal advisor in the Kimberley Process Certification Scheme. She has also worked as a General Manager Legal Services for the Zimbabwe Land Commission.

Steve Mberi is a Research Fellow with the Sam Moyo African Institute for Agrarian Studies (SMAIAS) and Administrator and Editorial Assistant of the Agrarian South: Journal of Political Economy (Sage, India). His research interests lie in the field of climate change, land, natural resources management, environmental policy and planning. His current research work has been focused on capital and climate change politics, with specific reference to smallholder tobacco farmers in Zimbabwe. He holds an MSc in Development Studies from the National University of Science and Technology (NUST).

Terence M. Mashingaidze is a Senior Lecturer in the Department of History and the Executive Dean of the Faculty of Arts at the Midlands State University in Zimbabwe. He has a PhD in History from the University of Minnesota, USA, and an MA in African History from the University of Zimbabwe. He has published on dam-induced displacements, nationalism and reconciliation processes in post-colonial Zimbabwe. He is a former Social Science Research Council (SSRC) - Africa Peacebuilding Network (APN) research grantee.

Francis Muromo is a Research Fellow with the Tugwi Mukosi Multidisciplinary Research Institute (TMMRI) of the Midlands State University (MSU). He holds a PhD in Rural Resource Management from University of KwaZulu Natal (UKZN), an MPhil in African Studies from the University of Cape Town (UCT) and an MSc in Rural and Urban Planning from the University of Zimbabwe. His research interests are in rural development, particularly rural livelihoods and dynamics behind sugarcane out grower schemes in the aftermath of Zimbabwe's land reform.

Chrispen Maseva is an environmental and social sustainability practitioner with over 23 years' experience of working with both rural and urban communities. Between 1997 and 2003 he worked for the then

Department of Natural Resources as an Ecologist responsible for the Environmental and Social Impact Assessment policy and process. He became the Chief Ecologist in 2005, soon after the transformation of the Department into the Environmental Management Agency (EMA). In 2006 he joined the Zimbabwe Electricity Transmission and Distribution Company (ZETDC) as its Chief Environmental Planner and was involved with applying the African Development Bank's Integrated Safeguards System (ISS) in relocation and compensation processes for transmission line construction projects. Currently, he is the Chief Environmental Expert at the Infrastructure Development Bank of Zimbabwe (IDBZ). He holds an MSc in Environmental Policy and Planning from the University of Zimbabwe.

Joel Chaeruka is a Lecturer in the Department of Rural and Urban Planning at the University of Zimbabwe. He is an experienced planner who worked for the Ministry of Local Government Public Works and Urban Development, Department of Physical Planning, as Chief Planning Officer in the Midlands Province and Mashonaland East Province before becoming the Deputy Director responsible for strategic planning. He holds an MPhil and MSc in Rural and Urban Planning from the University of Zimbabwe and his academic interests are in planning law and practice, urban development and management, urban design and settlement systems.

Christof Schmidt is the Advisor for Advocacy, Research & M&E at the Centre for Conflict Management and Transformation (since 2017). He is a development practitioner who has been working with Weltfriedensdienst e.V. (WFD) in international development cooperation and peace-building since 2013 and joined the Civil Peace Service (CPS) programme in Zimbabwe in 2015. He has an MA in Political Science and Philosophy from Leibniz University Hannover, Germany.

Shadreck Vengesai is the Research & Advocacy Coordinator at the Centre for Conflict Management and Transformation (since 2017). He is a development practitioner with over 10 years' experience working for local, regional and international non-governmental organisations and has an LLM in International Human Rights Law from Tilburg University, Netherlands.

Foreword

Ambassador Mary S. Mubi

The Government of Zimbabwe's Vision 2030 is an ambitious, transformative and inclusive development agenda to achieve an "Empowered and Prosperous Upper Middle-Income Society by 2030".[1] Vision 2030 will be realised through the implementation of successive national development strategies.

The development agenda outlined in the 'National Development Strategy 1' is underpinned by key clusters which include economic growth and stability; food and nutrition security; structural transformation and value chains; infrastructure, utilities and digital economy; housing delivery; human capital development; health and well-being; image building, internal engagement and re-engagement; devolution and decentralisation; and the cross cutting issues: youth, sport, culture and gender mainstreaming; financial inclusion; social protection, poverty alleviation and safety nets; governance; environmental protection, climate resilience and natural resource management.

These priority clusters were identified within the context of the United Nations' Sustainable Development Goals (SDGs), the Regional Indicative Strategic Development Plan (RISDP) of the Southern African Development Community (SADC) and the African Union's Agenda 2063. The above-named context ensures that the country mainstreams the goals and key priorities of the United Nations, African Union and SADC.

The development agenda prioritizes inclusive growth, with the devolution process providing a mechanism for provinces to plan and prioritize development projects that take advantage of the comparative and competitive advantage of each province whilst ensuring that the people remain at the centre of development.

---

1 Government of Zimbabwe (2020). *National Development Strategy 1*, January 2021 – December 2025. Harare: Government Printer.

Around the world, large-scale development projects providing critical infrastructure and enhancing natural resource exploitation for economic growth have all too often been associated with the negative social impact of internal displacements of rural communities. In Zimbabwe, the devolution process provides an opportunity to improve such development projects and mitigate negative impact by incorporating elements of a bottom-up approach. The different ways in which such projects are planned, and the mechanisms put in place for consultation with local communities, are crucial in minimizing the degree to which communities may be negatively affected.

The book provides a timely opportunity for stakeholders, including government ministries, local authorities, development partners, researchers, and civil society, to have a conversation about the social and economic impact of development-induced displacements in Zimbabwe and to reflect on the past and present experiences and practices. In order to learn from our past, we need to document past experiences and analyse them. The detailed case studies in this book provide crucial evidence that will inform future practices.

Zimbabwe's history of planned displacements is part and parcel of the colonization process. Colonial efforts to develop infrastructure, agriculture and mining within a racially segregated society were anchored in the displacement of the indigenous African people into native reserves. Their social and economic livelihoods were deliberately disrupted in order to serve as a source of cheap labour for the colonial settlers. The long-lasting negative effects of these developments on the local communities are still deeply felt in many areas of Zimbabwe.

Independence ushered in significant strides in the introduction of more inclusive governance structures and social and economic development in order to address inherited inequalities caused by successive colonial governments. It remains imperative to envision and implement a robust development agenda to re-address inherited inequalities with respect to access to infrastructure and housing, whilst at the same time ensuring that large-scale development projects directly benefit local communities, mitigate negative impact of displacements and prevent marginalisation of the affected people.

Furthermore, whilst the land reform programme significantly improved access of indigenous people to land, lack of security of tenure has also resulted in some communities being exposed to multiple successive displacements thereby limiting the potential for sustainable agricultural investments.

There is therefore a need to interrogate the legal, regulatory and administrative frameworks to ensure the protection of communities that may be affected by present and future large-scale developments. In this regard, it is important for the country to be guided by our own constitution and accompanying legal and administrative frameworks, as well as regional, continental and global best practices, and to ensure that we adhere to international conventions to which we are signatory.

The researchers and writers of this book present very compelling reasons for comprehensive reforms and alignment and implementation of legal frameworks and administrative processes that prioritize the improvement of project planning, impact assessments, community consultation, budgetary provisions for relocation and/or compensation of affected communities, and clarity in the demarcation and responsibilities of various institutions in land management and administration.

I wish to thank the Centre for Conflict Management and Transformation and the Tugwi Mukosi Multidisciplinary Research Institute for this important initiative and those who contributed to this book for their valuable contributions. These contributions are relevant for Zimbabwe and beyond our borders.

As we embark on the first five years of the 'National Development Strategy' towards the country's Vision 2030 which prioritizes inclusive growth, our expectation is that this book and its recommendations will receive the attention of all stakeholders.

Introduction

Tugwi Mukosi Multidisciplinary Research Institute

Development projects, natural disasters and wars can trigger internal or international population displacements. According to Gebre (2003), some population movements are voluntary whereas others are involuntary. The World Commission on Dams (2000) points out that displacement is an unintended negative externality of development projects. Smith (2002) in concurrence with de Wet (2006) opined that displacement by development projects is the single largest cause of involuntary migration in the world. Cumulatively, development projects rather than war cause the greatest population movement (Robinson 2003). Whereas in recent years drought and civil wars in Africa have received widespread coverage as fundamental causes of population movement, development projects are increasingly taking over as the major cause of current challenges being faced by some local communities today.

The inception of these development projects is often marked by political grandstanding with emphasis placed on the need for trade-offs between meeting national socio-economic developmental targets and debt servicing rather than on the welfare of development impacted communities. Globally, in the last 25 years there has been increasing recognition that the number of involuntarily development displaced people has become a problem that warrants investigation (Gebre 2003; Robinson 2003).[1] Whereas the Southern African Development Community (SADC) member states have only 2% of the world's population, they are home to 10% of displaced people in the world (SARPN 2006). Displacement exacts social, environmental and economic costs on exceedingly vulnerable and marginalised communities with tenuous and variable livelihoods (Thukral 1992: 51; Cernea 1997).

---

1 See also "The Violence of Development (Balakrishnan Rajagopal)", *The Washington Post,* 8 August 2001.

Introduction

This book on development-induced displacements in Zimbabwe unpacks the underexplored risks and vulnerabilities encountered by affected communities in different parts of the country. Such threats include socio-economic and environmental factors that aggravate people's vulnerabilities to hunger, disease and structural marginalisation (Adger et al. 2014). The policy relevant book also critiques Zimbabwe's legal architecture and regulations governing development-induced displacements (DIDs) in both the colonial and post-colonial periods, as well as proffering alternative safeguards for protecting people from the negative implications of the arbitrariness common to the country's development processes. From the construction of the hydro-electric power generating Kariba Dam in the 1950s to the post-colonial emergency of the irrigation water supplying Osborne and Tugwi-Mukosi[2] dams, Zimbabwe's celebrated artificial water bodies have been iconic representations of state initiated development projects that inevitably put human welfare at risk.

Paradoxically, the Kariba Dam was spearheaded by an exclusionary colonial government, while Osborne and Tugwi-Mukosi dams were post-colonial government initiatives. This shows that in spite of the differing ideological orientations of Zimbabwe's successive governments, the impact of dams on project affected people (PAPs) has been consistently negative largely due to weak legal and regulatory safeguards for DIDs. Besides disrupting water flows, creating new disease ecologies and reconfiguring landscapes, these dams triggered massive displacements, disrupted daily routines, fractured social relations, and relegated women's socio-economic standing.

The Kariba Dam triggered the displacement of 57,000 Gwembe-Tonga people in both Zambia (34,000) and Zimbabwe (23,000) from the Zambezi riparian, where they had practiced secure and livelihood sustaining flood recession agriculture. The colonial government relocated the Tonga to the arid, dry and wildlife and tsetse fly infested abutting uplands of Binga District. From that point on the Tonga have been struggling with a precarious existence as food insecure people dependent on donor largesse and occasional support from the ever negligent national governments.

Tugwi-Mukosi Dam caused the displacement of 18,000 people in 2014. The government haphazardly relocated these people to the congested and disease prone Chingwizi Transit Camp, where they lived for more than six

---

2 The Tokwe-Mukosi dam was renamed Tugwi-Mukosi dam in 2018, see "Tokwe-Mukosi renamed Tugwi-Mukosi", *The Herald*, 24 March 2018.

months. These relocatees subsequently moved to the camps' hinterland, where they were settled on inadequate one hectare plots without any security of tenure (Hove 2016). Furthermore, in 2005 an urban renewal project code-named Operation Murambatsvina (or Operation Restore Order) displaced 700,000 people in Zimbabwe (Tibaijuka 2005).[3] In Manicaland, about 600 households have been displaced to pave way for diamond mining in Chiadzwa (Madebwe et al. 2011) and approximately 1,600 households for the development of the Chisumbanje bio-ethanol plant in Chipinge (Thondhlana 2014). In all these cases, displacees became enmeshed in a vicious cycle of poverty, powerlessness and socio-economic marginalisation.

In unpacking the complex and long-term impacts of development-induced displacements (DIDs) in Zimbabwe, this book deploys Michael M. Cernea's "Impoverishment, Risk and Reconstruction (IRR) Model" (Cernea 2000). The model shows that physical displacement triggers concomitant social and economic exclusion of the affected groups. This results in eight impoverishment risks of landlessness, joblessness, homelessness, marginalisation, increased morbidity, food insecurity, loss of access to common property, and social disarticulation. These risks are inescapable because displacement entails land expropriation and asset dispossession. In fact, resettlement "de-capitalizes the affected population, imposing opportunity costs in the forms of lost natural capital, lost man-made physical capital and lost social capital" (Cernea 2008, p.5). The logic in the IRR Model is that if those who plan relocation and compensation processes take cognisance of or anticipate the aforesaid risks, the displacees' impoverishment can be minimised. Though synergistic, these risks do not manifest in equal intensity, they are context specific.

Research questions

The book intends to address the following main research questions:
1. What synergistic risks and vulnerabilities did Zimbabwean communities encounter due to development-induced displacements?
2. Which approaches and models have been utilised by the responsible authorities in Zimbabwe in terms of relocation and compensation?

---

3   Although the 'Operation Restore Order' cannot be classified as development-induced displacement and needs to be interpreted in its political context, it also points towards challenges in urban development resulting in evictions.

3. How can Zimbabwe reconfigure its laws and regulatory frameworks governing development-induced displacements and land tenure security?

Chapter outline

The *first section* includes a historical overview of development-induced displacements in Zimbabwe, a study of the Zimbabwean legal framework protecting the rights of displaced people, as well as an analysis of Zimbabwe's complex land tenure systems in the context of displacement processes.

Hon. Chief Ngungumbane unpacks Cernea's IRR model as a conceptual tool for identifying the intrinsic risks that cause impoverishment through involuntary displacement. He presents an overview of development-induced displacement cases in colonial and post-independence Zimbabwe, while emphasizing the impact on the affected people. He recommends improved planning processes to protect the rights and livelihoods of displaced people, and pleads for a stronger role of communities and traditional leaders in the planning and implementation of development projects.

Thammary Brenda Vhiriri analyses how and to what extent relevant Zimbabwean laws, legal and administrative instruments comply with the provisions of the Kampala Convention in terms of protecting internally displaced people, in particular small-scale farmers and rural communities, from arbitrary displacement through land acquisition for developmental projects. She recommends a stand-alone law and institution to address the specific issues faced by internally displaced people, as well as realigning relevant laws in order to ensure comprehensive consultations with the affected people and to protect the land rights of rural communities and beneficiaries of the land reform programme.

Steve Mberi analyses land tenure insecurity as an aggravating factor for displacements of rural communities in Zimbabwe. He discusses the fundamentals of the Zimbabwean multi-form tenure system and the challenges to land tenure security especially of rural communities, including the specific vulnerability of women in terms of land dispossession. He also explores current land struggles in the context of the dominating neoliberal model of development and focuses on displacements by commercial projects that are eroding the livelihoods of the peasantry in Chiadzwa and Chisumbanje in Manicaland Province. He recommends strengthening land administration systems, gender-sensitive approaches and community participation in decision-making as a way to improve land tenure security and prevent unjustified displacements.

The *second section* consists of two case studies on development-induced displacements during the colonial era. The case studies analyse the relocation and compensation processes undertaken by colonial administrations and the long-lasting legacy of those displacements, which negatively affect the displaced people until today.

Terrence M. Mashingaidze conducts a comparative analysis of the Northern and Southern Rhodesian governments' Kariba Dam induced displacements of the Tonga in their respective domains. He argues that the Northern Rhodesian colonial administration engaged the Tonga through the Gwembe Native Authority in planning for the displacees' compensation and putting in place mechanisms that guaranteed some benefits from the emerging Lake Kariba, while the Southern Rhodesian native affairs officials simply ordered the Tonga on their side of the Zambezi to relocate without compensation and adequate planning for decent livelihoods in the adjoining uplands.

Francis Muromo explores the experiences of two headmen in Zaka District in Masvingo Province resulting from the displacement of one headman and his community by the construction of Bangala Dam on Mutirikwi River and the establishment of commercial cattle and game ranches for white farmers in Chiredzi District. The study focuses on the negative impact of the forced migration on livelihoods and the long-term conflicts that emerged from the influx of displaced persons into the host community.

The *third section* consists of case studies on development-induced displacements that occurred after independence. The case studies analyse how relocation and compensation processes were handled by the responsible authorities, how they affected the displaced people and which lessons can be learnt from those experiences.

Chrispen Maseva compares the resettlement and compensation processes of the Marovanyati and Causeway dam projects. As key factors negatively affecting the process he identifies failure to include relocation and compensation costs in the total project budget, delayed relocation and compensation until the end of the project, poor coordination between the responsible authorities, lack of alternative land for displaced people, and lack of direct benefits of projects for the local people.

Joel Chaeruka investigates urban sprawl as a major challenge causing displacements of inhabitants of rural land. He unpacks the Zimbabwean legal framework on urban development in rural areas and presents the results of a study carried out in Mazowe District in Mashonaland Central Province on the nature of urbanisation, forms of displacement, how these displacements are being mitigated, and which challenges arise in terms of compensation, including compensation for tangible cultural heritage.

Christof Schmidt and *Shadreck Vengesai* outline the challenges rural communities experience when they have to cede land to pave way for development projects. Based on case studies in three districts of the Midlands Province, they analyse the impact of the relocations on the affected communities and the strengths and weaknesses of the different approaches used by the local authorities in terms of consultations and negotiations, resettlement on alternative land, compensation for improvements and disturbances, and rehabilitation of social, economic and cultural development.

References

Adger, N. W. et al. (2014). "Human security", in C. B. Field et al. (eds), *Climate Change 2014: Impacts, Adaptation and Vulnerability. Part A: Global and Sectoral Aspects*. Cambridge/New York: Cambridge University Press.

Cernea M. M. (1997). "African Involuntary Population Resettlement in a Global Context", Social Assessment Series, Environment Department Papers, World Bank.

—— (2000). "Impoverishment Risks and Reconstruction: A Model for Population Displacement and Resettlement", in M. M. Cernea and C. McDowell (eds), *Risks and Reconstruction: Experiences of Resettlers and Refugees*. Washington DC: World Bank.

—— (2008). "Reforming the Foundations of Involuntary Resettlement: Introduction", in M. M. Cernea and H. M. Mathur (eds), *Can Compensation prevent Impoverishment: Reforming Resettlement through Investments and Benefits Sharing*. New Delhi: Oxford University Press.

De Wet, C., ed. (2006). *Development-Induced Displacement: Problems, Policies and People*. New York: Berghahn Books.

Gebre, Y. (2003). "Resettlement and the Unnoticed Losers: Impoverishment Disasters among the Gumz in Ethiopia". *Human Organization*, 62(1), pp.50-61.

Hove, M. (2016). "When Flood Victims became State Victims: Tokwe-Mukosi, Zimbabwe", *Democracy and Security*, 12(3), pp.1-27.

Madebwe, C., V. Madebwe and S. Mavusa (2011): "Involuntary Displacement and Resettlement to Make Way for Diamond Mining: the Case of Chiadzwa Villagers in Marange, Zimbabwe", *Journal of Research in Peace, Gender and Development*, 1(10), pp.292-301.

Oliver-Smith, A. (2002). "Displacement, Resistance and the Critique of Development: From the Grass-roots to the Global", RSC Working Paper No. 9, International Development Centre, University of Oxford.

Robinson, C. W. (2003). "Risks and Rights: The Causes, Consequences, and Challenges of Development-Induced Displacement", Occasional Paper, The Brookings Institution - SAIS Project on Internal Displacement.

SARPN (2005). "Regional Meeting on Refugees and Internally Displaced Persons in the Southern African Development Community (SADC): Background Paper", Southern African Regional Poverty Network.

Thondhlana, G. (2014). "The Local Livelihood Implications of Biofuel Development and Land Acquisitions in Zimbabwe", Africa Initiative and Centre for International Governance Innovation.

Thukral, E.G., ed. (1992). *Big Dams, Displaced People: Rivers of Sorrow, Rivers of Change*. New Delhi: Sage Publications India.

Tibaijuka, A. M. (2005). "Report of the Fact-Finding Mission to Zimbabwe to assess the Scope and Impact of Operation *Murambatsvina*", United Nations Special Envoy on Human Settlement Issues in Zimbabwe.

World Commission on Dams (2000). *Dams and Development*. London: Earthscan Publications.

Key Issues and Recommendations

Centre for Conflict Management and Transformation

In 2019, the Centre for Conflict Management and Transformation (CCMT) hosted a series of multi-stakeholder policy dialogues on the issue of development-induced displacements in Zimbabwe. In addition, a research symposium was held in collaboration with the Tugwi Mukosi Multidisciplinary Research Institute (TMMRI, Midlands State University) on Zimbabwean displacement experiences and policy options. This book, with contributions from researchers and practitioners, is a result of that process.

Rural communities, particularly in developing countries, face perpetual risks of being displaced by infrastructure development projects (e.g. dams, roads, transmission lines), urban development and expansion projects, or large-scale commercial projects (e.g. mining, timber and agribusiness). Development-induced displacements may lead to loss of land, livelihoods, shelter, property, and access to social facilities, natural resources and cultural heritage, if the affected people are not cushioned by appropriate compensation and social support mechanisms, as well as integrated rehabilitation programmes to mitigate negative impact. As a result, communities often resist relocations and in some instances the emerging conflicts between the responsible authorities and the affected communities delay critical development projects.

The policies of the Government of Zimbabwe are geared towards rural development, economic growth and foreign investment. This calls for a complementing review and harmonisation of legislation, policies and practices designed to protect the rights and livelihoods of rural communities affected and displaced by development projects. During the course of the policy dialogues and research symposium, the following four main areas of concern and key recommendations were identified to mitigate negative impact and conflicts caused by development-induced displacements in Zimbabwe.

1. Free, prior and informed consent (FPIC)

Relocation and compensation of people to pave way for development projects should be guided by the principle of FPIC: "In plain terms, FPIC is knocking on somebody's door and asking for permission before you come in" (Portalewska 2012, p.15). Free implies the absence of coercion, intimidation and manipulation. Prior means that consent is sought in advance of the development project that will result in physical or economic displacement. This includes the time necessary to allow the affected people to undertake their own decision-making processes. Being informed means that the affected people have been provided all information relating to the development project and that the information is objective, accurate and presented in a manner and form understandable to them. Consent implies that the affected people have agreed to the development project that will result in their physical or economic displacement based on the compensation processes and packages that have been negotiated with them. The FPIC concept goes beyond mere involvement; it entails the meaningful participation of people who will be affected by a development project in the processes that lead to the making and designing of such a project.

Key recommendations:

- To give sufficient public notices and conduct public consultations and hearings in which affected communities are also informed about their rights.
- To negotiate the terms and conditions of relocation and compensation with the affected people or their chosen representatives and any relevant third party.
- To reimburse expenses of the affected people for legal or other representation and any documentation they require.
- To make any agreement available in written form to all involved parties and stakeholders.

2. Fair and comprehensive compensation

Compensation refers to financial payments, replacement of structures and assets, or any other form of support received by the affected people in order to compensate them for any damages or losses they reasonably incurred due to the displacement. Compensation is guided by the principle of equivalence: affected people should be neither enriched nor impoverished due to the process (FAO 2008, p.24). However, an improvement of their situation is desirable.

In terms of immovable assets of the affected households (buildings, sanitation, fencing, irrigation, fruit trees, crops etc.), compensation should be determined and negotiated based on an independent and transparent valuation process. If the affected people are physically relocated from one place to another, transport should be provided for any movable property. Disruptions of the economic activities and livelihoods of the affected people should be mitigated as much as possible and factored into the compensation package.

Even though the affected people may not own the land they occupy and use, they usually have a right to being allocated alternative land (i.e. occupants of communal land). In the case of rural households, agriculture is in most cases the main source of livelihoods. Therefore the easiest way to rehabilitate livelihoods is resettlement on alternative arable land suitable for agricultural production. If such agricultural land is available, the land size and quality should at least be equivalent to the land they occupied and utilised before. In order to avoid tenure insecurity, multiple relocations and additional costs for the affected people, the allocated land should be adequately assessed, developed and registered by the responsible authorities.

Key recommendations:

- To conduct or commission valuation assessments of immovable household assets.
- To inform affected people about the process and methods of the valuation and to provide the option of making own submissions if feasible.
- To replace buildings and other improvements based on the principle of equivalence or to provide material support and/or financial compensation that enables equivalent replacement.
- To take reasonable measures for mitigation of disruptions and disturbances.
- To provide technical and material support and/or financial compensation for any disruptions, disturbances or other damages reasonably incurred due to the process.
- To allocate equivalent or better land to the affected people that is at least as suitable for the intended occupation and use as the previously held land.

- To facilitate allocation and registration of land and to waive registration and development fees.
- To fairly compensate any affected people who are lawfully settled on the land in question (including customary law), to treat illegal settlers in a humane manner, and to consider informal settlers as formal if their settlement has been condoned by the authorities for an extended period.

3. Inclusive socio-economic development and profit-sharing schemes

Even if affected people are not physically relocated from one place to another, they may still be economically displaced as a result of the development project affecting their livelihoods, way of life and socio-economic rights. An example of economic displacement is the loss of agricultural fields or access to commons, such as grazing land, forests, water sources, and fishing grounds, as a result of development projects, such as mining, urban development or dam construction. Environmental pollution by mining activities may also render arable land unproductive, which results in economic displacement of communities that surround mining sites.

In the case of urban development or expansion in rural areas, affected rural households are sometimes offered to be incorporated and to receive urban residential stands as alternative land. However, this may still put them at risk of being economically displaced by losing agricultural land as their main source of subsistence and income. In such cases, the affected people may need additional facilities and support enabling them to access alternative means of livelihoods (e.g. providing additional stands, employment opportunities, exemption from fees and levies, flea market stands, mining claims, fishing rights, market gardening, small plots under irrigation, or inclusion in education support programmes, such as the 'Basic Education Assistance Module'). When designing compensation models and packages, adequate response mechanisms to economic displacement must be factored in to achieve sustainable development.

If the affected people are physically relocated, in some instances they may lose access to natural resources and commons, public infrastructure and services, cultural heritage sites, and social facilities (e.g. water sources, forests, grazing land, business centres, roads, dip tanks, veterinary and agricultural extension services, cemeteries, schools, clinics). This might particularly affect vulnerable groups, such as school children, elderly and people with disabilities or health issues. Therefore it is crucial to develop, implement and monitor comprehensive resettlement plans that guide the relocation process and ensure that the new location is sufficiently prepared and developed for human settlement and rehabilitation of livelihoods in advance of relocations.

In order to avoid loss of access to resources, infrastructure, facilities or services, any responsible authority for development projects which result in any kind of displacement should conduct or commission comprehensive 'Environmental and Social Impact Assessments' (ESIAs), which are supposed to inform resettlement and compensation plans. Where a development project does not satisfy ESIA requirements, the responsible authorities should suspend the funding and implementation of the project until such time these requirements are fulfilled. This will assist in reducing adverse social and economic consequences of development projects on the affected people.

Projects that displace local people should be designed in a way that provides direct benefits and opportunities for the local people, which may not be restricted to mere employment. In the case of large-scale mining and hydroelectric projects or any other public or private projects that have a commercial component and generate profits, compensation models should not be designed as a once-off facility and community shareholding should be considered. The responsible authorities should set up transparent and accountable profit or dividend sharing schemes to enable the affected communities to continuously derive benefits and investments into local development from the project that displaces them.

Key recommendations:

- To provide, support and enable alternative sources of livelihoods and/or access to social support programmes, if equivalent alternative land for agricultural production is not available.
- To commission ESIAs on the social, economic, cultural, and environmental impact of the project on the affected people and to develop, implement and monitor comprehensive resettlement and compensation plans.
- To ensure equivalent or better access to public infrastructure and services, social facilities, commons and natural resources in the case of physical relocation.

- To identify and preserve important cultural heritage sites, to provide the option of reburials and to consider and facilitate culturally relevant processes, such as rituals.
- To design transparent and accountable shareholding and profit sharing schemes benefiting the socio-economic development of displaced communities.

4. Relocation and compensation before project implementation

Internationally, it has increasingly become a standard practice and requirement for funding and loan facilities to assess the environmental and social impact of development projects and to set aside sufficient funds and facilities for relocation, compensation and socio-economic rehabilitation of the affected people. Multilateral financial institutions, such as the World Bank and African Development Bank, do not want to be associated with negative social impact and human suffering as a result of development projects they are supporting and facilitating.

However, the planning and management of some development projects by some public and private institutions in Zimbabwe is still mainly concerned about the financial viability, technical implementation and potential revenues of such projects, while potential negative social impact often remains an afterthought. When the total costs of development projects are estimated and budgeted, costs for relocation and compensation are either not included or there are no mechanisms and facilities in place to ensure the timely availability and accessibility of adequate funds to conduct the necessary processes before the project implementation.

There are several examples where the affected people received compensation several years after development projects have commenced or even after they had been completed. As a result, the value of financial compensation was eroded by inflation. After two decades, government is yet to complete compensating people displaced by Tugwi Mukosi dam.[1] Therefore it becomes crucial to assess the environmental and social impact and to budget for relocation and compensation costs at the planning stage of development projects.

Before approving and commencing development projects that will require relocation or compensation of affected people, a comprehensive resettlement and/or compensation plan must be put in place and agreed upon with the affected people. Funds and facilities should be set aside for

---

1 "$1.5 million for Tokwe Mukosi dam flood victims", *Newsday*, 29 May 2019.

completing relocation and compensation processes within the agreed upon time frames and a technical committee should be tasked with monitoring the progress. If such processes and agreements are not being adhered to, the development project should not be approved or funds for the implementation of the project should not be released.

Key recommendations:

- To factor relocation and compensation costs into development project plans and budgets at the planning stage.
- To create specific funds and facilities designated for the implementation of relocation and compensation processes before commencement of a project.
- To clearly outline the payment schedule, the currency and mode of payment, as well as interest rates applicable to delayed payments in any agreement involving financial compensation.
- To complete the replacements of crucial structures and infrastructure at the new location and to pay at least partial compensation in advance of relocations.
- To avoid 'red tape' and intermediaries and provide compensation to the beneficiaries directly through the project if feasible.
- To ensure that any third party benefiting from a development project contributes towards relocation and compensation of the affected people in a transparent and accountable manner.

Conclusion

Development must not be associated with human suffering. Instead, development must bring with it inclusive progress and positive transformation to societies. To minimise negative impact of development projects and conflicts between the affected people and the responsible authorities, we recommend to all stakeholders to facilitate free, prior and informed consent, to ensure comprehensive and fair compensation for land, improvements and disruptions based on transparent valuation processes, to minimise economic displacement by conducting environmental and social impact assessments and planning towards rehabilitating livelihoods and socio-economic development, as well as incorporating community shareholding and profit-sharing schemes. To that end, relocation and compensation costs should be included in development project budgets and adequate plans, mechanisms, budgets, funds, and facilities should be established to ensure timely completion of relocation and compensation processes as part of the project implementation.

References

FAO (2008). "Compulsory Acquisition of Land and Compensation", Land Tenure Studies 10, Food and Agriculture Organization of the United Nations.

Portalewska, A. (2012). "Free, Prior and Informed Consent: Protecting Indigenous People's Rights to Self Determination, Participation and Decision Making." *Cultural Survival Quarterly*, 36(4), pp.14-17.

I

PERSPECTIVES ON HISTORY, LAW AND POLICY

Development-Induced Displacements in Zimbabwe: A Historical Overview and General Experiences of the Affected People

Hon. Chief Ngungumbane

1. Introduction

Development is one of the activities undertaken by government and communities which has a fundamental bearing on their political, economic and socio-cultural landscape. Development initiatives have led to the establishment of various infrastructures like dams, clinics, schools, hospitals, bridges, among many others. However, some development programmes have resulted in the displacement of people from one place to the other, in most cases against their will and consent. This chapter will discuss development-induced displacements which have taken place in the rural areas of Zimbabwe and will present a critical analysis of the impact on the affected people.

There are two types of displacement: primary or direct displacement and secondary or indirect displacement.

(i) *Primary/direct displacement*

Primary displacement occurs when people are moved from their traditional lands to make way for a development project. This is planned for and can be controlled to a certain degree.

(ii) Secondary/indirect displacement

Secondary displacement occurs as a result of environmental, geographical and socio-political consequences, such as natural disasters and wars. Such displacements are less predictable and difficult to control. Secondary displacement is the most prevalent and prominent among the two forms of displacement.

2. Cernea's 'Impoverishment, Risk and Reconstruction Model' (IRR)

Cernea's model was developed in the late 1990s and provides a conceptual tool for identifying the intrinsic risks that cause impoverishment through involuntary displacement and resettlement (Vivoda et al 2017). Cernea identifies eight potential risks of displacement.

Figure 1: Cernea's model of displacement

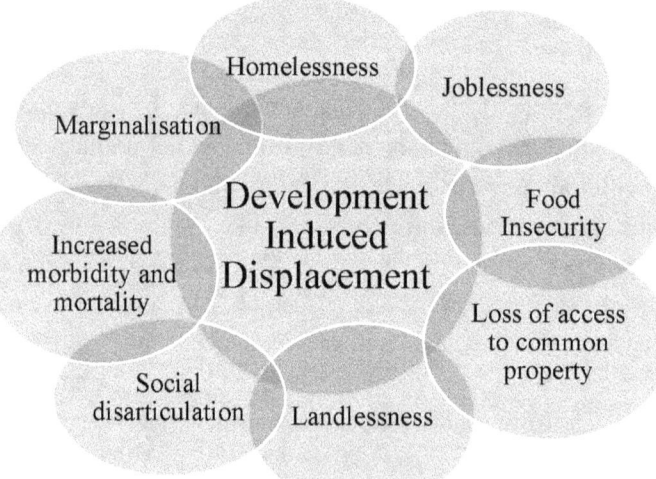

Landlessness

- Land is the main foundation on which many people build productive systems, commercial activities and livelihoods. Land is vital for developing food production, business enterprises and provision of services.
- Land is pregnant with natural resources like gold, diamond, platinum,

gas, and many others. Activities related to the exploitation of those resources have resulted in the displacement of people and animals.
- International and traditional standards require that productive systems including land are compensated or replaced at full value.
- Land is a finite resource which would be scarce over time and could result in landlessness of affected people, once development-induced displacement programmes take effect.

Joblessness

- When people are involuntarily resettled, the risk of losing access to employment is high.
- In the rural areas, employment can be both formal and informal and displacement and resettlement can cause the loss of either. Sectors normally affected include agricultural workers, extension workers, service workers, and miners.
- Development-induced displacement in most cases takes away sources of livelihoods.

Homelessness

- Homelessness occurs when there is no or inadequate compensation for those people who are being resettled or displaced and if there is no alternative land and houses provided after the displacement.
- Homelessness also occurs if the extended family system associated with African families is not taken into consideration. Subsequently, the provision of smaller and single-family homes could leave some family members displaced and homeless.
- Provision of sub-standard housing increases future risks of homelessness since it increases the risks of the destruction of homes through natural disasters and inclement weather.

Marginalisation

- Marginalisation occurs when displaced persons lose economic power and experience a reduction in social status and confidence.
- Relative economic deprivation and marginalisation begins prior to physical displacement, such as when investments, infrastructure and services in affected areas are discontinued in preparation of project commencement.
- Marginalised people have very little or no access to the justice systems in the likelihood that their human rights have been violated. Such human rights include the first, second and third generation rights.

- First generation rights (civil and political) include the right to life, human dignity, personal security, equality and non-discrimination, political freedom, freedom from slavery and servitude, freedom of movement, and residence rights.
- Second generation rights (economic, social and cultural rights) include labour, freedom of profession, trade and occupation, health care, food and water, and education rights.
- Third generation rights (collective human rights) include rights to natural resources, development, peace, communication, shared heritage, and a healthy environment.
- As a result of displacement, people lose their forms of livelihoods and this can cause stress-related illness. Domestic violence becomes prevalent in such instances and cases where the father is the bread-winner.
- Such marginalised people are vulnerable and become easy targets for manipulation in return for money and in worst scenarios beer.

Morbidity and mortality

- Displaced and resettled people can be affected by stress and trauma due to their experiences of loss, powerlessness and sudden fundamental changes in their way of life.
- Affected people can be exposed to parasitic and vector-borne diseases, such as malaria, and diseases associated with inadequate shelter or the poor choice of resettlement location. Unsafe water supply and unsanitary conditions can increase vulnerability to epidemics and chronic conditions, such as diarrhoea and dysentery.
- Children, infants, elderly, disabled, and (pregnant) women are the worst affected.

Loss of access to common property

- Resettled people often lose access to common property, such as grazing lands, forests, woodlands, coastal and inland water bodies, and burial grounds.
- Displacement can result in the destruction of graves, which is a taboo in the African culture. Loss of graves and burial grounds will result in the loss of connectivity and attachment with the supernatural world.
- Displacement can result in the failure of the indigenous people to carry out their rituals, as the new owners would not be prepared to allow the displaced people to come back for those rituals (trespassing on private property).

Food insecurity

- Food insecurity occurs when persons are displaced from their land or sources of livelihoods and as a result do not have access to sufficient, safe and nutritious food and water in order for household members to live active and healthy lives.
- Replacement land can be of lesser productive value than the land previously occupied and utilised or it can be located in areas with low rainfall and prone to droughts, which will result in hunger, starvation and even deaths.
- New settlement areas can also be located further away from services and resources that households depend on for additional food supplies, such as markets.

Social disarticulation

- Social disarticulation describes the fragmentation of communities through weakening cohesion, informal networks and interpersonal ties among displaced persons.
- Fragmentation occurs as a result of poorly designed and managed displacements, which result in the dismantling of social organisation, support systems and interpersonal ties among displaced persons.
- Social disorganisation results in the displacement and dismantling of established institutions of power and leadership, such as traditional leadership.

Development-induced displacement is necessitated by development projects for mining, electrification, water bodies, roads, urban development, among many others. All governments across the world have eminent-domain powers, meaning that governments, within the confines of the laws of each country, have powers to move people from any area identified as a priority area earmarked for development. Eminent-domain extends to the security establishments, such as military barracks, installations and training facilities. It is important that the state does a thorough cost-assessment of the development activity versus the impact. Cost-benefit-analysis must be done first and community involvement is of paramount importance. The benefits of the development must accrue to the community and country at large.

3. Examples of development-induced displacements in the colonial era

In Zimbabwe, the challenge of development-induced displacements started before the colonial era and was more pronounced during the colonial era, where the settler regime removed traditional leaders from their areas of jurisdiction to areas which were unfamiliar to them and less arable. Chiefs and their people were displaced in order to accommodate farming and mining activities which the government of the day prioritised over the general welfare of the locals. Chiefs like Ngungumbane were displaced from Esigodini in Matebeleland South Province to Mberengwa in Midlands Province, while Chief Fish Gwebu was displaced from Matebeleland South to Buhera in Manicaland Province. Chief Shana and his people were moved from Masvingo Province to the Jambezi area of Matebeleland North Province. The Karanga people were moved from the Chivi and Bikita areas to the Shangaani dominated areas of Chiredzi in the Masvingo Province and Gokwe in the Midlands Province. Chief Ruya and his people were moved from Chirumanzu District and resettled in Silobela in Kwekwe District, among many others.

Such displacements created conflict as movement created language, traditional and cultural barriers among the displaced people and the inhabitants of the areas where they were resettled. Forced migration led to a loss of connection to historical, religious, symbolic or spatial locations and diminished cultural identity. The colonial government used development-induced displacement programmes to destroy the cultural, social and traditional fabric of the indigenous people of Zimbabwe. It is important to note that during the colonial period the government-initiated development programmes brought both positive and negative impact. Positive impact was realised in the construction of infrastructure like dams, clinics, hospitals etc., which brought benefits to the community. Negative impact derived from the fact that those people who were displaced were not consulted and their forced movement to other areas led to the loss of their land and traditional and cultural connections.

This assertion is supported by Bakare (1993, p.46), who emphasizes that "land is a place of connection with mother earth, where one's roots are, where one's umbilical cord has been buried, where one's ancestors are deposited, a place of connection and orientation". The movements of traditional leaders identified above resulted in the loss of their ancestral land, the traditional and cultural rituals associated with the land, and more importantly the natural resources.

Some of the notable displacement programmes that took place include the construction of the Kariba Dam in the late 1950s and early 1960s, which led to the displacement of the Tonga people living on both sides of the mighty Zambezi River. Lake Kariba is 223 km long and up to 40 km wide. Families along its stretch were displaced to make way for the water body. Displacements also took place in other areas along the 2574 km long Zambezi River, which covers a number of countries in the Southern African Development Community (SADC) region.

People were relocated to areas they were not familiar with, e.g. Chief Ngezi who was displaced and resettled in Mhondoro-Ngezi. The river and subsequent lake were their sources of livelihood, as the river offered resources and jobs to the locals and improved their socio-economic status. However, the locals have not fully benefitted, while people from far away areas gained from fishing and subsequent employment of non-locals in the lucrative industry. The centralisation of services has made it difficult for locals to access fishing permits which are acquired in Harare. Such marginalisation has been a recipe for conflict.

The displacement by the Kariba dam construction resulted in a loss of the Tonga's cultural sites and traditional rituals. The river god of the Tonga called 'Nyaminyami' became separated from his people. Chiefs along the mighty Zambezi River have complained about the loss of their economic livelihoods and their disconnection from their ancestral spirits. The chiefs believe that the 'Nyaminyami' was responsible for the many losses of lives that occurred during the construction of the dam, as this was done without the consultation and blessing of their ancestral spirit.

The second major example of development-induced displacement occurred as a result of the establishment of transmission lines and electricity pylons, which moved power from Kariba to different parts of the country. What is particularly disappointing is that the majority of the displaced people have not benefitted from the electricity that passes close to their homes. The fortunate ones who have electricity in their homesteads are subjected to long periods without power and the question is whether they have derived any benefit from the relocation from their original homes. Many lost their fields which were their source of livelihoods, while some have even lost their lives and livestock as a result of lightning emanating from the pylons.

The third major example is the displacement and resettlement that took place at national parks. The main debate and argument is whether the animals or people were displaced in order to accommodate the other. National parks like Hwange, Mana Pools, Rhodes, Matopos, Gonarenzhou or Chizarira necessitated movements of people in order to accommodate animals and vice-versa. The question is whether the adjacent communities have benefitted from the proceeds through initiatives like the Zimbabwe's Communal Areas Management Programme for Indigenous Resources (Campfire). Such displacements and resettlements have been accompanied by human-wildlife conflicts, which have witnessed the injury and death of animals and human beings. Chief Mvuthu, Shana, Nekatambe, Nelukoba, Mola, Mvuthu, Dandawa, Chitanga, Sengwe, Binga, Tshovani, Siphoso, Mathuphula, Matsiwo, Chisunga, Chapoto, among many others, have endured human-wildlife conflicts.

4. Examples of development-induced displacements in post-independence Zimbabwe

In post-independence Zimbabwe, several prominent incidents of displacements took place, including the displacement of people by the construction of the Insukamini Dam in the Lower Gweru area under Chief Bunina in the late 1980s. People were relocated from their original homes to new areas by the Vungu Rural District Council and the construction of the dam affected the original route followed by the road from Gweru to Maboleni. Some of the locals have benefited from irrigation schemes which are a source of employment and livelihood.

Table 1: Examples of post-independence development-induced displacements

Chieftanship	District	Province	Nature of displacements
Bunina	Gweru	Midlands	Construction of Insukamini dam
Mataga	Mberengwa	Midlands	Construnction of Mundi-Mataga dam
Mathupula	Tsholotsho	Matabeleland North	Over-flooding of the Gwayi river

Chieftanship	District	Province	Nature of displacements
Chivi, Chitanga	Chivi, Mwenezi	Masvingo	Construction of Tugwi-Mukosi dam
Musikavanhu, Garahwa	Chipinge	Manicaland	Chisumbanje Sugar plantation
Zimunya, Marange	Zimunya	Manicaland	Chiadzwa diamond fields

In the case of the Mundi-Mataga Dam in Mberengwa District, a feasibility study was conducted which identified households to be relocated. However, a second phase was necessitated as a result of poor feasibility study results in the initial stage and this forced a further 88 families to be displaced as a result of the rising waters from the dam. Nonetheless, some locals have benefited from irrigation which has led to employment and improved livelihoods.

In Tsholotsho, families adjacent to the Gwayi River were relocated as a result of the flooding river in Tsholotsho. The government provided land and promised to provide further amenities. Some of the affected families received decent houses, which had incomplete toilets. However, some families never received these houses and were accommodated in tents, which have since been damaged. Some of these families have since returned to the river banks of the Gwayi River due to lack of water, arable land, essential amenities, and pastures for their animals. While this example is not directly a development-induced displacement and more closely linked to natural disasters, it illustrates the importance of adequate planning, provision of all essential amenities, and the payment of full compensation prior to displacement.

Another prominent example is the construction of the Tugwi-Mukosi Dam in Masvingo Province, which displaced more families than any other single displacement case since independence. The affected people were moved to places that did not have infrastructure and sanitation services. The displaced families accused government of not fully compensating them initially and offering low compensation in the subsequent events.

The expansion of the mining sectors created further risks for rural communities to be displaced. The Ministry of Mines and Mining Development has declared 'Exclusive Prospecting Orders' (EPOs) for certain areas which means that those areas become protected and people will be forced to relocate once the prospecting orders are granted. Often EPOs are used for speculative purposes and there is no adequate cost-benefit analysis taking into account that displacements of people will result in loss of livelihoods, social disarticulation, marginalisation, and food insecurity, as propounded by the IRR model.

The Communal Land Act highlights that communal land is vested in the state through the president. Therefore, rural communities occupy the land on the benevolence of the state which legally owns the land. Traditional leaders with their communities have limited bargaining powers for fair compensation, once they are relocated to new areas. To compound this, cultural and social rights are violated and livelihood projects are halted as communities are moved to new areas without the requisite infrastructure to resemble or promote their economic activities.

In Chiadzwa in Manicaland Province, Chief Marange, Chief Zimunya and their subjects were involuntary relocated from their original homes to pave way for diamond mining companies and had to resettle in faraway areas with poor infrastructure. Although they were provided houses, the houses soon showed fatigue as a result of poor workmanship. The people of Marange and Zimunya and the region at large did not derive many benefits from companies that are mining diamonds in Chiadzwa. Some of the companies mining diamonds did not fulfil their pledges of supporting the Marange-Zimunya Community Share Ownership Trust which resulted in lack of financial capitalisation of the Trust and low levels of development in areas where people were resettled. The people of Manicaland and beyond have complained about the lack of benefits from natural resources in their areas. Calls for devolution of power have grown louder as a result of the lack of development and failure to develop infrastructure for people affected by displacement.

In Chisumbanje, the chiefs and their people had their cultural and social rights violated and livelihood projects halted because the communities were moved to new areas to pave way for the construction of the new bio-ethanol plant. Konyana (2014, p.4) describes the sad scenario when Chief Garahwa and Chief Musikavanhu, interviewed between 12 January and 27 March 2013, agreed on the negative impact with their headmen Mahanye, Sumbanje, Takawira and Machona. They gave a detailed explanation which the author captures in their language:

Hatirambi budiriro munharaunda yedu. Budiriro chiro chakanaka yaamho ngekuti tinobetsereka maningi. Chokutanga, vana vedu vanoona mishando, vosiya kunzerereka vachiita zvisina shwiro. Chechipiri, tinoonawo zvekushandisa semapato, mvura yekumwa yakachena, makiriniki uye zvikora. Asi panotinesa ngepekuti budiriro yacho inounzwa pakati pedu tisingabhuyirwi ngezvayo. Semunomu, takangangoona muyungu uyu Macdom aunzwa ngeARDA, ozwi ndiye aakutora minda yeshe yatainge nayo kuti arime nzimbe dze ethanol. Pasina nguva, takaona paakuvakwa fekitori ye ethanol kuchitorwa vanhu vekuretu kuti vashande. Minda yeshe yatairima magwere esadza netonje rekutengesa yakatorwa. Atisisina pekurima kuti tizviraramise. Sakei teiti iyi budiriro yakatipa dambudziko uye atisi kudakara ngezvayo. Pamusoro peizvi, makuwa evasharukwa vedu aasisina unongwarira. Nendau dzetaitira zvechivanhu chedu dzave pamhene.

We are not against development. Development is a good thing for it helps us a lot. First, our children get jobs and stop loitering and being mischievous. Secondly, we get utilities such as roads, clean drinking water, clinics and schools. But where we are troubled is when development is brought in our midst without consultation, our knowledge and involvement. As in this area, we just saw a white man Macdom who was brought by ARDA to occupy all the land we had so that he grows sugar-cane for ethanol. In no time, a factory was built with labourers being hired from faraway places. All the land we used to grow maize for our subsistence and cotton for sale was taken away. Now we do not have land to cultivate maize for self-sustenance. That is why we are saying this development project brought problems and we are not happy with it. In addition, the graves of our ancestors have no one to look after them now. Our sacred shrines where we used to hold our traditional ceremonies have been exposed.

Adjaye and Misawa (2006) highlighted that in an African setup nothing happened without the knowledge of the traditional leader. For most of the cases indicated here and elsewhere, there has been little consultation between stakeholders and traditional leaders. It is crystal clear that development is fragmented and not well coordinated. Section 282(1)(c) of the Constitution of Zimbabwe identifies the facilitation of development as one of the fundamental roles that the traditional leaders must undertake. This therefore means that chiefs must be involved in the development process in their areas of their jurisdiction, as those engagements will bring meaningful and sustainable development.

From the examples above there is little engagement with traditional leadership structures and their people. This is further evidenced by a recent conflict involving chiefs in the town and villages adjacent to Lake Kariba, who have raised concern over alleged side-lining of local labour in the USD $294 million Kariba Dam plunge pool reshaping project.[1] This scenario dovetails the IRR Model where locals are being side-lined in development processes taking place in their area.

A recent documentary produced by Zimbabwe Environmental Lawyers Association (ZELA) in conjunction with ActionAid Zimbabwe[2] reveals that 27 households in Vhimba in South Chimanimani in Manicaland Province received a 72-hour eviction notice from the Zimbabwe Parks and Wildlife Management Authority (ZimParks) for allegedly encroaching into a natural conservancy igniting a dispute with a long history. A landmark judgement handed down by the High Court of Zimbabwe stopped ZimParks from evicting the Chimanimani banana farmers, which sets a precedent that development-induced displacements can be challenged. Development is expensive and so are relocations which call for a concerted effort in the planning and implementation of the development agenda. In the planning scenario, it is important to take cognisance that land is a finite resource which one day will become scarce thus further complicating the matter of displacing people for development.

The other challenge is that the various pieces of legislation dealing with development, relocations, compensation, and the roles and responsibilities of stakeholders are not harmonised and realigned. An example is Section 282 of the Constitution of Zimbabwe which gives chiefs the role of facilitating development, while Section 60 of the Rural District Councils Act provides for the establishment of the 'District Development Planning Committees' whose membership consists only of technocrats, including the following: security organs of the district, district development coordinators, chairpersons of every other committee established by the council, the chief executive officer of the council, district heads of each ministry, departments of a ministry.

1   "Chiefs, Kariba pool project planners lock horns", *The Herald*, 4 November 2019.
2   Available at: https://actionaid.org/stories/2019/threat-community-vhimba

This committee is critical as it considers ward development plans and makes recommendations to the full councils as to matters to be included in the annual development and other long-term plans for the district where the council is situated. This is where the issues of development-induced displacements are likely to be discussed and plans will be done. Ironically, these issues also fall into the jurisdiction of the chief concerned, whereas a chief is also expected to play a critical role in the development agenda of his area. While chiefs sit in councils, they are mere *ex officio* members who do not have voting rights and are not allowed to sit in council committees, although this is where most of council business is conducted.[3]

5. Recommendations

- There is need for harmonisation between different pieces of legislation and policies that relate to development and development-induced displacements. Such processes should be guided by a clear home-grown compensation and rehabilitation policy and framework to cushion communities that need to be relocated to pave way for development.
- There is need to realign government legislation and policies which relate to the Exclusive Prospecting Orders (EPO), as mining is set to generally take precedence over agriculture and other related sectors.
- While ownership of communal land is vested in the president, locals must take ownership of natural resources through their traditional leaders in their areas, so that they have the power of bargaining when new projects take place in their areas.
- Locals must negotiate and become shareholders in new projects that come into their areas and they are able to negotiate through relevant arms of government for a fair adequate compensation and relocation allowance. This has been done by the Royal Bafokeng Trust in Rustenburg, South Africa, and by the Ashanti Kingdom of Ghana who have a joint partnership and ownership with AngloGold Ashanti with the locals as shareholders.
- This joint partnership entails a win-win partnership where all partners benefit and there is no partner who loses out. This will enable the mandatory construction of economic and social infrastructure and the development of sources of livelihoods before and after relocations.
- Compensation must be paid before relocations occur and it must

---

[3] This is different in parliament where chiefs have voting powers and sit in parliamentary committees.

include the betterment of people's livelihoods and living standards. Amenities like roads, schools, houses, hospitals and clinics must also be put in place in advance of relocations.
- Proper planning by relevant authorities must cater for potential displacements. There is need for councils and other stakeholders to carefully plan for future development-induced relocations. Project planners must identify poverty risks associated with involuntary resettlement. It needs to be determined whether district, provincial, national, regional or private authorities must cater for current and future displacements and any related costs must be included in the relevant budgets.
- Traditional leaders must be involved in the development agenda of their areas of jurisdiction and proper consultation and planning must be done with indigenous people at all stages of development and natural resource extraction. Locals represented by their traditional leaders must be directly engaged by public and private institutions, organisations and companies which bring development projects in their area.
- Locals must be consulted and involved in the traditional, social, cultural, human, and environmental impact assessments of the potential development in their area in a language they understand. Communities and all relevant stakeholders need to be trained on the issues, laws, rights, and challenges related to development-induced displacements.

References

Adjaye, J. and B. Misawa (2006). "Chieftaincy at the Confluence of Tradition and Modernity: Transforming African Rulership in Ghana and Nigeria", *International Third World Studies Journal and Review*, XVII, pp.1-10.

Bakare, S. (1993). *My Right to Land, in the Bible and in Zimbabwe*. Harare: Zimbabwe Council of Churches.

Government of Zimbabwe (2013). *Constitution of Zimbabwe Amendment (No. 20) Act*. Harare: Government Printer.

—— (2002). *Rural District Councils Act, Chapter 29:13*. Harare: Government Printer.

—— (2002a). *Communal Land Act, Chapter 20:04*. Harare: Government Printer.

Konyana, E.G. (2014): "Why Development-Induced Displacement is Morally Objectionable: An Ethical Appraisal of the Macdom-ARDA Chisumbanje Ethanol Project in Chipinge, Southeastern Zimbabwe." *Greener Journal of Philosophy and Public Affairs*, 1(1), pp.1-6.

Vivoda, V. et al (2017). "Applying the Impoverishment Risks and Reconstruction (IRR) Model to Involuntary Resettlement in the Global Mining Sector", Workbook, Centre for Social Responsibility in Mining, Sustainable Minerals Institute, University of Queensland.

2

Development, Land Acquisition and Displacement: An Analysis of the Extent of the Compliance by the Laws of Zimbabwe to the Kampala Convention

Thammary Brenda Vhiriri

1. Introduction

The global community has become conscious of the suffering and specific vulnerability of 'Internally Displaced People' (IDPs). The gravity of their situation is a source of continuing instability and tension for states and affects their socio-economic development. This has necessitated the definition of internal displacement and the search for durable solutions towards IDPs. An appropriate and specific legal framework for the protection and assistance of IDPs became an urgent need. Hence African states at their Special African Union Summit in Kampala, Uganda, on 23 October 2009 joined hands on the cause and adopted the African Union Convention for the Protection and Assistance of Internally Displaced Persons in Africa (Kampala Convention), which came into force on 6 December 2012.

In November 2013, Zimbabwe became one of the first countries in Africa to demonstrate commitment to a legally enforceable framework on IDPs by appending its signature to ratify the treaty. This chapter follows up on the progress Zimbabwe has made, seven years down the line, in putting up the appropriate legislation and policy provisions to comply with the provisions of the Kampala Convention. It focuses specifically on development-induced displacements due to infrastructure development, urban expansion and mining. Special attention is given to the security of land tenure systems, the right to compensation, reinstatement or otherwise resettlement, and IDP's right to be consulted and appeal in the context of development projects.

1.1. Key terms

- *Human settlement*: It is comprised of a human group and the habitat of this group, not just the roads, houses and other infrastructure, but also the sets of social relationships. They are wide-ranging covering such issues as population, pollution, employment, social welfare, health, food, and shelter (Overseas Development Institute 1999).

- *Internal displacement*: This means the involuntary or forced movement, evacuation or relocation of persons or groups of persons within internationally recognised state borders.

- *Development-induced displacements:* These are involuntary internal displacements caused by infrastructure, industrialisation, electrification, mining, and urbanisation processes arising out of large-scale and capital-intensive development projects (Robinson 2003).

- *Land rights:* They include the right to undisturbed occupation of a homestead or land for annual and perennial crop growing, permanent improvements, burials, and gathering fuel, poles, wild fruit, thatching grass, minerals etc.; transactional rights in terms of giving, mortgage, lease, rent, and bequeathing areas of exclusive use; at the same time the right to exclude others from enjoyment of the same rights at community and/or individual levels; and access to legal and administrative provisions in order to protect the rights holders.

- *Land tenure:* It refers to the terms and conditions, on which land is held, used and transacted (Adams, Sibanda and Turner 1999). Tenure refers to the rules, relationships and institutions that define rights of ownership in and access to landed property (ZHRNGOF 2010).

- *Land tenure reform:* It is the systematically planned changes to the terms and conditions of tenure in order to address a range of problems arising from settler relocation and dispossession (Adams, Sibanda and Turner 1999).[1]

---

[1] Land tenure reform must be built on a thorough understanding of the livelihood strategies of those intended to benefit based on a rural participatory approach as opposed to rapid rural appraisal.

- *Public purpose:* According to section 2 of the Land Acquisition Act, this includes a purpose that is necessary or expedient in the interests of defence, public safety, public order, public morality, public health, town and country planning, or the development or utilisation of any property in such manner as to promote the public benefit or the economic wellbeing of the community.
- *Resettlement models in Zimbabwe:* In the Fast Track Land Reform Programme, Model A1 was intended to decongest communal lands. Settler selection and emplacement for A1 was the responsibility of the provincial and district officers. Model A2 was aimed at the creation of indigenous commercial farmers on a full cost recovery basis from the beneficiary. Settler selection was through applications to the Ministry of Lands, Agriculture and Rural Resettlement (Utete 2003). With the above cited definition it should follow that resettlement areas are not necessarily the communal lands.

2. Land tenure in Zimbabwe prior to and after the land reform

In their studies, Adams, Sibanda and Turner (1999) postulated that Zimbabwe inherited a highly skewed pattern of land distribution with 1% of farmers holding nearly half the available agricultural area and the bulk of the fertile land. According to the Utete Report (2003) land acquisition for speculative purposes was the precursor to land acquisition for agricultural production as an economic activity, its euphemism being 'white agricultural policy' which commenced in 1908. However, its successful realisation was predicated on the continued dispossession of indigenous Africans of their best land and the destruction of their property in the years 1908-14.

The vast majority of indigenous African farmers were confined to designated 'Tribal Trust Lands' and traditional leaders responsible for customary land allocation within those areas. Post political independence, the Communal Land Act of 1982 shifted the authority from the chiefs to district councils and to 'Village Development Committees' (VIDCOs). However, in 1996, cabinet accepted the advice of the Rukuni Commission (1994) that this should be reversed. Though the commission's recommendations were endorsed, the resources needed at that time for the formalisation of village boundaries were yet to be made available.

In reference to sections 3, 5 and 6 of the Communal Land Act's Part II, communal land consists of land which previously was under 'Tribal

Trust Land'. Subsequently, any minister through secondary legislation, such as a statutory instrument, can designate any land areas as communal land. Only when there has been consultation with a Rural District Council and at the same time a proposed law that shall develop into a statutory instrument, can part of communal land cease to be. When read with the Communal Land Act's Part III (occupation and use of communal land), it is made clear that even though according to the Regional, Town and Country Planning Act anyone may occupy and use communal land for agricultural and residential purposes, there has to be consent first sought from the Rural District Council and if not granted, an appeal may follow. Upon the first application, the Rural District Council consults further with the customary law relating to the allocation, occupation and use of the land in the area concerned and cooperates with the chief of the community as per the Traditional Leaders Act.

In the context of the land reform based on the willing seller – willing buyer provision, government managed to acquire 3.5 million hectares and resettled 71,000 households between 1980 and 1990. However, the communal areas still remained congested, overstocked and overgrazed thus pressure militated on the government to accelerate its land reform programme. The subsequent fast track land reform process created A1 (small-scale) and A2 farms (medium-scale commercial). It allowed that over 15,000 new A2 farm rights and about 140,000 A1 farm rights be allocated (Moyo 2006).

The land reform exercise provided government with an opportunity to revisit land tenure systems. Tenure reforms introduced new tenure regimes with 99 year leasehold contracts for A2 farms and settlement permits for A1 farms. However, according to Sachikonye (2005, p.37) land and tenure reforms paid "little attention to the 200,000 farm worker households who were displaced by the process". This failure undermined opportunities for farm workers to gain access or be allocated quotas to resettlement land. Consequently, some newly settled A2 farmers have resisted mandatory granting of residency rights to former farm workers in their farm compounds in preference of only having the current employees on their farms.

The granting of leasehold title implemented the recommendations of the Utete land committee that the issue of leases or other forms of legal title for the beneficiaries of the A2 model be concluded speedily as this would assure the productive use of the land, the quantum of individual lease rentals and other cost recovery measures. Also recommended had been the urgent addresses of the situation of former farm workers in the farm compounds of former white commercial farmers whose continued presence was creating numerous problems that included illegal gold panning, misuse of farm facilities and resources, and general criminal activities.

3. Kampala Convention

This treaty made provisions for displaced people from their settlements due to a variety of factors. Cited below are Articles III and X of the Convention. The expectation is that member states will implement its provisions in order to effectively deal with the issue of internal displacement of persons.

> *Article III*
> *General obligations relating to States Parties*
>
> States parties shall:
>
> a) Incorporate their obligations under this Convention into domestic law by enacting or amending relevant legislation on the protection of, and assistance to, IDPs in conformity with their obligations under international law;
>
> b) Designate an authority or body, where needed, responsible for coordinating activities aimed at protecting and assisting IDPs and assign responsibilities to appropriate organs for their protection and assistance, and for cooperating with relevant international organisations or agencies, and civil society organisations, where no such authority or body exists;
>
> c) Adopt other measures as appropriate, including strategies and policies on internal displacement at national and local levels, taking into account the needs of host communities;
>
> d) Provide, to the extent possible, the necessary funds for protection and assistance without prejudice to receiving international support;
>
> e) Endeavour to incorporate the relevant principles contained in this Convention into peace negotiations and agreements for the purpose of finding sustainable solutions to the problem of internal displacement.

Article X
Displacement induced by projects

1. States parties, as much as possible, shall prevent displacement caused by projects carried out by public or private actors;
2. States parties shall ensure that the stakeholders concerned will explore feasible alternatives, with full information and consultation of persons likely to be displaced by projects;
3. States parties shall carry out a socio-economic and environmental impact assessment of a proposed development project prior to undertaking such a project.

It is clear from the wording of the treaty that there is a deliberate move to treat internal displacement as a stand-alone issue which should not be lumped up together with other basic human rights. In Zimbabwe, people are displaced for development purposes, such as to pave way for dam, road or railway constructions, mining projects, and urban expansion, as government or local authorities seek to deliver public goods.

Initially, development was seen as a necessary evil wherein people were forced to relocate in order to transform from traditional to complex and modernised societies. The initial processes, especially under colonial rule and before independence, were detached from a people-oriented perspective. While the beneficiaries are numerous, the costs tend to be borne disproportionately by the poorest and most marginalised groups of the population. Displacement causes socio-economic and cultural disruption by breaking up living patterns and social continuity. It dismantles existing modes of production, disrupts social networks, causes the impoverishment of many of those uprooted, and threatens their cultural identity.

4. Zimbabwean legal instruments and policies in the context of the Kampala Convention

4.1. Zimbabwe's drive for infrastructure development and exploitation of natural resources

Like many other developing countries, Zimbabwe has been on a drive for major infrastructure development and improvement of its macro-economic stability using both medium- and long-term plans, e.g. the Economic and Structural Adjustment Programme (ESAP) 1991-1995, the Zimbabwe Programme for Economic and Social Transformation (Zimprest) 1996-1998, the Short Term Emergency Recovery Programme

(STERP) 2009-2013, the Zimbabwe Agenda for Sustainable Socio-Economic Transformation (ZIMASSET) 2013-2018, and the Transitional Stabilization Programme (TSP) 2018-2020. For instance, government and private sector efforts have sought to improve the mining sector in order to ensure that resources are exploited more effectively of which citable is the then President in 2014 (Zimbabwe Medium Term Plan 2011-2015, pp.137-139), who said the following:

> In pursuit of a new trajectory of accelerated economic growth and wealth creation, my Government has formulated a new plan known as the Zimbabwe Agenda for Socio-Economic Transformation (ZIMASSET): October 2013 - December 2018. ZIMASSET was crafted to achieve sustainable development and social equity anchored on indigenisation, empowerment and employment creation which will be largely propelled by the judicious exploitation of the country's abundant natural and human resources.

The series of Zimbabwe's economic policies indicate that there is a dire need for economic growth and development. However, especially the exploitation of natural resources can negatively affect local communities and the livelihoods of small-scale farmers in ways which they may never recover from. The economic blue print policies were not inclusive in nature, as they were formulated by the executive with insufficient engagement of the people who were going to be directly impacted by the proposed development.

An example is the Marange diamond extraction in Chiadzwa, wherein several hundred households were displaced to pave way for what was regarded as an organised way of mining. The Government of Zimbabwe together with some foreign private investors decided to mine for diamonds in the Chiadzwa mining fields, as opposed to the villagers who were panning on the diamonds fields. It should be noted that the majority of the affected families were relocated to Arda Transau farm. It has to be acknowledged that the houses that were built for them at the relocation site were much better than their clay homesteads. However, issues of the proximity to health and education facilities still needed to be addressed.

The desire for development is further reinforced in section 13 of the 2013 Constitution of Zimbabwe which provides for national development. This section goes further to make it mandatory for government departments to include 'the people' in the formulation and implementation of development plans. Though this section does not expressly refer to internally displaced people, the Constitution of Zimbabwe by implication makes it mandatory for affected people to be involved throughout the process of the proposed development. The section further expressly protects the rights of women and children. One of the human rights enshrined in the Constitution of Zimbabwe is that of protection from deprivation of property, which asserts that no property of any description can be compulsorily acquired or taken away except under the authority of the law. However, a person having any right or interest in compulsorily acquired land for the land reform programme has no right to challenge the acquisition in court, but can appeal against the issue of compensation.

It would appear that these provisions of mandatory consultative processes are not fully implemented for one reason or another on both the administrators' and affected persons' part. The absence of a fully assigned institution to protect the interests of IDPs results in the lack of awareness of the existence of such enshrined rights. It is also important to note that most of those affected by development projects are local communities and small-scale farmers in the communal areas and A1 resettlement schemes. Although they may know their rights, they often lack resources or understanding on how to protect their rights.

4.2. Land acquisition for mining

It would be ideal as desired by the Kampala Convention that there be a stand-alone legislation to protect the rights of internally displaced people. A specific IDP law would to a greater extent provide a degree of legal certainty hence making it easy for government agencies to implement its provisions. The absence of a specific Act of Parliament to protect IDPs leaves a huge gap if, for instance, the provisions of the Mines and Minerals Act, Section 31 (1)(g)(i-iii) are to be considered. This section makes it mandatory for a prospective miner to seek consent from the owner of land whose farm is less than 100 hectares, before the commencement of any mining activity. Unfortunately, this is also taken away on Section 31(1)(g)(iii) which empowers the Minister of Mines to exercise his discretion to disregard the land owner's choice of not giving consent for mining activities to take place on his farm. There is no room for arbitration or presentations by the farmer who faces the risk of being displaced due to the size of their land. In most cases the mining activities bring along with them other social implications such as the number of workers, who will naturally bring their families on site.[2] The farmer is forced to adjust to the new social-cultural norms, relations and ills brought in by the neighbouring miner and workers. Should the farmer be outnumbered, sometimes the relationships may turn out very sour rather than harmonious.

In this instance, there is no engagement of the farmer who may be totally or partially displaced. The discretion is left solely in the hands of the minister responsible for mines. This section may lead to worse circumstances for the current farmers under the prevailing land tenure system. The current mining legislation was enacted as far back as 1961 and has not been effectively amended to keep abreast with the changing environment, both within the mining sector and in national policy directions. The Mines and Minerals Act recognises private ownership of farming land, since this was the prevailing land title at the time of the enactment of the current Act when farming was pre-dominantly done by white farmers who had title deeds over farms. As such throughout the said Act reference is made to private ownership and the rights to claim compensation or to be bought out, which is only available to private owners. These rights were easy to enforce because the farmers could prove ownership. The Act has not been amended to ensure that those who possess the right to occupy and use the land are given the same privileges and rights as enjoyed by the previous holders of land titles.

The current land tenure system entails that land belongs to the state, while tenures such as the permit, offer letter and leases only give residents the right to occupy and use land. With all the discretionary powers left with the minister and land occupiers holding inferior titles which are not recognised by the current mining legislation, it becomes easier for people to be displaced in order to pave way for mining activities. This situation makes the current farm occupiers weak in their negotiations for compensation. It may turn out to be difficult for them to get compensation for the value of lost land because the said value belongs to the state. It gives investors excessive bargaining power to determine the value of compensation or even the place of resettlement.

Section 31(1)(h) provides that a prospective miner should get consent

---

2   For instance, the holder of a prospecting license has the right to take free of charge for primary purposes any public water or private water from land not closed to prospecting but only in so far as such taking does not interfere with the use of such water for primary purposes by the owner or occupier of the land.

over communal land from the Rural District Council of the area concerned. It does not make it mandatory for such council to have consulted the people to be affected by such a decision. Thus this gap usually results in office holders making decisions that are disconnected to the practicalities on the ground[3], while people in rural areas do not hold any tenure documents to resist the move or negotiate for better settlement. Section 26 of the Mines and Minerals Act regards every land, which includes state land, communal land and private land reserved to the Government of Zimbabwe, as open to pegging and prospecting, though the title held over such ground determines the negotiating strength of the affected parties.

There are several benefits that only land owners can enjoy, for example Part X and XXII and several other sections give more bargaining power to land owners. Thus the current tenure system as it exists is not acknowledged by the mining legislation, thereby disempowering particularly small-scale farmers without ownership rights who may be displaced due to mining. However, section 179 saves some of the rights of the landowner that include grazing of stock upon or cultivation of the surface area, as long as that is done without interfering with the proper working of the location for mining purposes. Furthermore, section 180 allows any approved cultivation scheme or proposed scheme relating to the owner or occupier of communal land situated on a registered mining location to lodge a complaint with the mining commissioner, provided an application in regard to the cultivation by such occupier of the whole or any part of the surface of such location is made.

4.3. Land acquisition and infrastructure development for regional de-concentration

On the other hand, the Regional, Town and Country Planning Act measures up to the notion of inclusivity, however, even these have their own shortfalls. Section 18 makes it mandatory for local authorities to consult and present their draft developmental plans to the public and wait for two months for objections from the public:

> In formulating, and before finally determining, the contents of a local plan, the local planning authority shall take such steps as will, in its opinion, ensure that there is adequate consultation in connection with the matters proposed to be included in the local plan.

---

3   This results in a top down approach as opposed to a bottom-up approach.

Though consultations have been made mandatory, the discretion still rests with the office holders to define what adequate consultations mean. Further the section does not make it mandatory for the consultation to be with the local people who may be affected by the proposed plan. The executive may decide to consult stakeholders and a small sample of local people as they deem fit and necessary. It can be argued that consulting of a small sample is not adequate and neither is there guarantee that the invitees are the ones directly affected by the proposed plan. This buttresses the need to have a stand-alone IDP law, so that officials are forced to follow it in letter and spirit and go to the actual areas to be affected by the proposed development.

Section 18(2)(b) of the Regional, Town and Country Planning Act also provides that the approved draft plan is subjected to public scrutiny by placing it in the public domain for at least two months before it can be endorsed as final. This also presents some gaps as most people in the communal areas hardly have time or resources to visit the offices of local authorities and read notice boards, unless they are advised and sponsored to do so. In the absence of civil society organisations that bring awareness programmes to the grassroots population, government and local authorities usually complain about a lack of resources to implement awareness campaigns or consultations. The end result is that the potential victims, who will pay the ultimate price for the proposed development, are left in the dark and only get to know about it when all the implementation wheels have turned and there is little or no room to seek further audience.

It is acknowledged that this Act of Parliament has put in measures to ensure that there are adequate consultations before development plans are put in place. However, there is need for the legislation to be more specific so as to reduce the discretionary powers that may be exercised by the executive and to protect the rights of potentially affected inhabitants. Furthermore, there is still a strong requirement as provided by the Kampala Convention for an assigned institution that will protect and push for set parameters for compensation, the process of appeal and possible reinstatement or otherwise resettlement.

According to the Regional, Town and Country Planning Act, land within the area of a local planning authority may be acquired for the implementation of any proposal, including development, redevelopment or improvement, contained in an operative master plan or local plan or an approved scheme.

However, the acquisition is done through an outright purchase, exchange, donation or other agreement with the owner of the land or expropriation or the imposition in a permit of a relevant condition. Section 46(2) underpins that where any land which is reserved for a particular purpose in an operative master plan or local plan or an approved scheme is to be acquired by expropriation, the local planning authority may, if so requested by the acquiring authority or the owner of the land concerned, issue a certificate stating the type of development or use which would have been permitted on the land and details of the conditions attaching. Any person dissatisfied with any such certificate issued is allowed to appeal within a stipulated period to an administrative court.

This is of particular relevance, since Zimbabwe is in a process of regional de-concentration based on growth pole strategies. In terms of section 264 of the Constitution of Zimbabwe this is referred to as devolution. In regional and urban planning terms, growth pole strategies, such as establishing urban centres and special economic zones in rural areas, are designed to reduce the level of regional concentration (Parr 1999), that is the extent to which metropolitan areas (Harare and Bulawayo) dominate the entire region (Zimbabwe) in terms of employment and population. Such internal urbanisation and urban expansion processes geographically are underpinned by section 45 and section 46 of the Regional, Town and Country Planning Act, which gives the local government the power to acquire or expropriate land for development purposes. This has the potential of displacing local inhabitants to pave way for the infrastructure that has to be built in order to support the devolution and growth pole strategies.

For instance, growth point boundaries were gazetted in 1982, however, some growth points initially did not develop as expected and local inhabitants were not resettled and land not cleared. While people were left settling within those boundaries and paid development levies to the councils, in the event of subsequent expansions under the devolution agenda such inhabitants and their families face the risk of being displaced as illegal settlers within gazetted boundaries.

On the other hand, the mushrooming housing cooperative societies in Zimbabwe may also present the nation with internal displacement challenges, especially if the Cooperative Societies Act (Chapter 24:05) is not realigned in order to deal swiftly with the rife land baronage cases. Furthermore, there are a lot of unregistered cooperatives that have been allocating land in the full view of local authorities. Land beneficiaries have constructed houses which they have inhabited for several years, only for the local authorities to demolish the said established communities on the grounds of non-authorisation. Surprisingly, construction inspections would have been done on the houses by officials from the said local authorities and while the settlers are being punished, both the local authorities and land barons or unregistered cooperative leaders go unscathed in this chaos. Measures have to be put in place so that local authorities are held accountable and are forced to act swiftly when they notice unauthorised activities within their boundaries.

A positive and specific provision to protect local inhabitants was enacted in the Environmental Management Act Section 110(1):

> Provided that no such area shall be set aside until the Minister responsible for the administration of the Communal Land Act [Chapter 20:04] is satisfied that suitable provision has been made elsewhere for the inhabitants who will be affected by the setting aside of the area.

This section makes it mandatory for alternative resettlement land to be put on the table before people can be moved to pave way for development hence protecting the rights of IDPs. Though resettlement on its own is not enough, the express provision in this section is a progressive legislative development. It is my considered view that a place to stay is the primary need, while all the other forms of compensation can be added on.

The Water Act in Sections 15, 16 and 17 also makes provisions for public notification of the authorities' plans. However, they have the same weaknesses as highlighted above that the said notices are displayed or published by means that are not readily accessible to the inhabitants to the extent that such notices do not effectively fulfil their purpose. It should be noted that the general trait in the respective legislation is that too much discretionary powers are left with the executive to have the final say after objections have been made by interested individuals.

Though the plans are done by technical personnel within a given institution, it is sufficient to say that the broader policy direction would have been given by the minister or permanent secretary of that institution. Therefore it would not be fair for the heads of these institutions to have the final say in deciding whether or not the proposed plans should be amended after receiving objections. It means that the only recourse that inhabitants will have are the courts, which intimidate most local rural people, and the time and monetary investment that is required could be out of their reach. There should be room for arbitration with a third party before a final decision is reached to ensure transparency and fairness in the conduct of such business.

So far the less progressive Act of Parliament is the Rural Land Act which in section 5 only requires that a notice of acquisition should be placed in a newspaper that circulates in the area of interest. Suffice to say that people in the rural areas hardly access newspapers. Furthermore, the Rural Land Act requires only people in whose name the land is registered or who have title deeds to make presentations against any acquisition. As it stands the majority of the local rural population are not registered and neither do they have any title deed to the land that they have occupied for generations. People from the rural areas have their names entered into a book by a headman for recognition and acceptance as part of the community, but do not hold any tenure document. It thus excludes these ordinary inhabitants from exercising their right to participate in any developmental plan, or it at least makes their negotiation power very marginal. To make it worse, this Act does not even make reference to the Land Acquisition Act which provides for the broader options and conditions for compensating displaced inhabitants. Thus its silence on issues of compensation and resettlement and its failure to recognise the prevailing tenure system in the rural areas entails that there is no intention to protect the rural inhabitants.

The Rural District Councils Act like the Rural Land Act fails to provide any form of inclusivity in the manner in which land can be acquired for development. Accordingly, land acquisitions and development processes risk being detached from the inhabitants, yet rural areas are the ones that are largely feeling the effects of development, especially with the issue of development now enshrined in the constitution under sections 13 and 264. In terms of section 78 of the Rural District Councils Act all that has to prevail is the desire of the minister to have development and everyone affected by such decisions will be compensated in terms of the Land Acquisition Act. The gap of lack of community participation exposes the population to arbitrary displacement, even when it is not really necessary.

4.4. Challenges in the context of the land reform

The Government of Zimbabwe phased its land reform programme into three phases, under which it also came up with the various tenure systems and decided to decongest the rural areas by resettling people into the freshly acquired farms using the A1 permit model. Under this model, individuals were supposed to occupy the farms as homestead/villagised model. Resettled persons could do their subsistence farming activities with a shared place for cattle grazing, though some of these A1 farms are self-contained. If this was meant to decongest the rural areas, it means that these people left behind their established communities to have a fresh start on the resettlement area, where they would further create new societal norms and values as they integrated.

Statutory Instrument 53 of 2014 came into effect to provide settlement permits for occupants who have been offered land in A1 resettlement areas, while also giving the Minister of Lands the power to cancel such A1 farming permits. However, there has been a backlog in the regularisation of resettlement schemes leading to non-issuance of those permits as tenure documents in many cases. Furthermore, another issue complicating the regularisation of resettlement areas and issuing of resettlement permits is that in some cases settlement patterns were not adequately planned. People resettled themselves or were resettled on former commercial farms at times beyond the carrying capacity of the land, which resulted in similar congestion and environmental challenges as in communal areas. In other instances, there is no adequate infrastructure for service delivery to accommodate the new settlement patterns on those former commercial farms. Therefore at times people have to be resettled again to decongest or to pave way for development of infrastructure, such as schools, clinics, roads, electrical grids, and other public goods.

Sections 19 and 20 of Statutory Instrument 53 of 2014 make it clear that once the minister has decided to acquire land, though the affected person is given 90 days to make objections, the decision would still rest with the minister to decide whether or not to terminate the permit. Section 20 provides for compensation and it is clear that inhabitants are only compensated for improvements made and for any crops that may be in the field. This scenario is very worrisome as these A1 permit holders were removed from their original places of habitat, their cultural norms and economic activities, as it was government policy to decongest the rural areas. They had to start afresh to rebuild their lives within the new resettlement areas, as this was a combination of people from various parts of the country who had to come together and find common cause.

There is no mandatory obligation on the part of the Minister of Lands to find alternative land for the person(s) whose permit will be terminated in the interest of the public as provided by this section. It should be noted that this leaves these individuals very vulnerable as they can no longer go back to their villages which by then would have re-adjusted boundaries in line with the prevailing population. Consideration should be made as to the extent of socio-economic disruption that is caused by these planned developments. There is need for a policy position to protect individuals from being displaced more than once, especially due to the fact that permit holders only have the right to occupy and use the land and therefore can be only be compensated for improvements and their crops, but cannot be compensated for the value of the land because the land belongs to the state.

Section 32 and 33 of the Land Commission Act gives too much discretionary power to the minister responsible for agriculture to evict certain groups or classes of individuals from a resettlement area. These sections leave a lot to be desired as there are two main classes of vulnerable groups from the land reform programme, namely the former farm labourers and former white farmers. The former farm labourers currently occupying some cottages within the re-allocated farms, without necessarily being employees of the new farm owners, are at risk. It should be noted that these groups of individuals have no tenure documents and have grown their families on the said farms at times up to the fourth generation. The longer government delays in addressing the issue, the more complex the situation will become as these people will eventually be in arms against the resettled farmers.

On the other hand, the majority of white farmers who have remained on the farms and have been allocated what is known as the 'remaining extent' are doing so without any tenure document, although like A2 beneficiaries of the land reform they have the option to apply for 99-year leases. Despite being allowed to continue farming on their allocated land since 2000, they continue to be displaced as and when it becomes necessary because they do not hold any tenure document. The existence of both these classes are recognised and acknowledged, yet they have no protection, in fact the executive is empowered to displace them without recourse.

Furthermore, the Zimbabwean government recently signed a Global Compensation Deal (GDC) with the former white commercial farmers on compensation for improvements on the land, but not necessarily compensation for compulsorily acquired land, as agreed in principle with the Commercial Farmers Union (CFU). Land related compensation is broadly a complex issue attaching to historical imbalances that this chapter shall not delve into in light of purpose and scope. Under Section 295 (compensation for acquisition of previously-acquired agricultural land) of the Constitution of Zimbabwe, indigenous farmers and farmers under Bilateral Investment Promotion and Protection Agreements (BIPPAS) must also be compensated for land taken over for the resettlement of A1 and A2 farmers during the fast track land reform programme. Statutory Instrument 62 of 2020 had to subsequently be gazetted to give effect to Section 295 and it paves way for previous land owners to apply for re-instatement of their previous farms in-lieu of compensation for previously-acquired agricultural land.

However, this is going to be difficult for the government to implement, since some of the beneficiaries of the land reform have been settled since 2000 and have adjusted their livelihoods and social integration accordingly, with some having established their grave sites within their new homes. Some of these A2 parent farms have between 5 to 20 resettled farmers and the numbers for A1 farms can go beyond 100 resettled families. The government will need sound financial resources to compensate the resettled farmers. Government also has to identify alternative land for the displaced settlers and this is increasingly becoming difficult as land is now scarce. Should any resettled farmers be displaced in terms of Statutory Instrument 62 of 20, it should be noted that these can only claim compensation to the extent that they are losing their right to occupy and use the land, and not as land owners. A set of criteria has to be in place as to which of the applicants in terms of the Statutory Instrument 62 of 2020 should be reinstated onto their farms and a clear and transparent strategy should be proffered as to how the displaced will be managed, in order to avoid too much discretionary powers being left to a few individuals.

5. Conclusion and recommendations

- *Lack of compensation other than for farm improvements*

  It is thus clear that under the current land tenure system which is largely based on leasing in its various forms, the land ultimately belongs to the state and the state retains the power to cancel title held under offer letter, 99-year lease, permits and other leases with or without an option to purchase. However, there is room for consultation with the Rural District Council in those instances when a minister wishes to issue out a statutory instrument that seeks to cease a habitation area as communal land. Constitutionally, there is no guarantee for alternative piece of land should one be displaced, for example, there is no guaranteed movement from resettlement land to communal land, but compensation for improvements on resettlement land is what can be expected. The Kampala Convention goes further by requiring state parties to provide other forms of reparations where appropriate, in addition to providing effective remedies to the persons affected by displacements.

- *Humanitarian assistance of IDPs*

  According to the Kampala Convention, IDPs should be availed humanitarian assistance in case of displacement. The land history of Zimbabwe shows that the colonial government had failed in this area and equally even the post-independence government had failed to observe this tenet in the fast track implementation of the land reform programme. The former farm worker group of IDPs arising from employment by former white commercial farmers has hugely been disadvantaged as a result and to date have not yet received adequate humanitarian assistance. Attention should be given to the recommendations of the Utete Report (2003) with regards to former farm workers.

- *Need for cooperation with other nation states*

  It is underpinned by the Kampala Convention that states shall cooperate with each other upon request of the conference of state parties in protecting and assisting IDPs. In Zimbabwe, the passing of the new 2013 constitution in which respect was given to BIPPAS is aligned to this. Similarly the passing of a Statutory Instrument 62 of 20 is highly likely in reference to the observation of this proposition from the Kampala Convention.

- *Consultations and prevention of displacements*

    With pieces of legislation such as the Communal Land Act that require consultations to first be done with the Rural District Councils, chiefs and customary laws in the event of intended implementation of development projects along the lines of the Regional, Town and Country Planning Act, it may follow that Zimbabwe is in default adherence to the Kampala provision that states shall prevent displacement caused by projects carried out by public or private actors. The consultations required by the Communal Land Act also fall in line with the Kampala Convention's requisition that state parties shall ensure consultation of persons displaced by projects leading to a bottom-up or participatory approach as opposed to imposition and top-down approaches of developmental projects. However, there is need for the legislation to be more specific in order to reduce the discretionary powers that may be exercised by the executive and to protect the rights of potentially affected inhabitants.

- *Environmental impact assessments (EIAs)*

    States are expected to carry out socio-economic and EIAs for any proposed development project prior to undertaking such a project. Zimbabwe has by default enshrined this requirement of the Kampala Convention in the Environmental Management Act.

- *No clear-cut dispute resolution procedures for IDPs to follow when aggrieved*

    It is also clear that there is little room for a less complicated manner of resolving disputes between the executive and objecting inhabitants. Too much discretionary powers is left with the executive to have the final say after objections have been made by interested individuals, whereas the Kampala Convention provides for an assigned institution that will protect and push for set parameters for compensation, the process of appeal and possible reinstatement or otherwise resettlement. It also should be noted with concern that though there are clear legal steps by government on how farms can be converted from farming to urban use between the Minister for Lands and the Minister for Local Government, neither the law nor the written policy addresses the issue of who should compensate the displaced farmers. The absence of a clear written position leaves the displaced farmers moving from office to office between the two ministries looking for a tangible recourse. It should be emphasised here that it is government practice to pre-warn settlers who are settled on known peri-urban farms that their allocation will be terminated in the future to pave way for the intended development. As such the above scenario applies in instances where the development had not been envisaged.

Recommendations are as follows:

- *Need for a specific IDP law*

  There should be a customised or stand-alone IDP law and institution that addresses specific issues affecting IDPs.

- *An independent IDPs representative body*

  A recognised body can continue to lobby for the interests of IDPs and ensure compliance. It can be said that the Government of Zimbabwe has progressively tried to provide for IDPs, but this is at a broad level using the general rights as provided by the Constitution of Zimbabwe.

- *Clear-cut reference points and standards*

  There is need to set clear parameters on valuations, compensation, the right to appeal, and engagements. Furthermore, there is need for an open platform for negotiation when there are objections to development, and the power to determine the outcome should not reside with the proposing authority but an independent third party.

References

Adams M., S. Sibanda and S. Turner (1999). *Land Tenure Reform and Rural Livelihoods in Southern Africa*. London: Overseas Development Institute.

Government of Zimbabwe (2020). *Statutory Instrument 62 of 2020, Land Commission (Gazetted Land) (Disposal in Lieu of Compensation) Regulations*. Harare: Government Printer.

—— (2018). *Land Commission Act, Chapter 20:29*. Harare: Government Printer.

—— (2014). *Statutory Instrument 53 of 2014, Agricultural Land Settlement (Permit Terms and Conditions) Regulations*. Harare: Government Printer.

—— (2013). *Constitution of Zimbabwe Amendment (No. 20) Act*. Harare: Government Printer.

—— (2005). *Co-operative Societies Act, Chapter 24:05*. Harare: Government Printer.

—— (2005a). *Environmental Management Act, Chapter 20:27*. Harare: Government Printer.

—— (2002). *Communal Land Act, Chapter 20:04*. Harare: Government Printer.

—— (2002a). *Land Acquisition Act, Chapter 20:10*. Harare: Government Printer.

—— (2002b). *Rural Land Act, Chapter 20:18*. Harare: Government Printer.

—— (2002c). *Rural District Councils Act, Chapter 29:13*. Harare: Government Printer.

—— (2002d). *Water Act, Chapter 20:24*. Harare: Government Printer.

—— (2001). *Traditional Leaders Act, Chapter 29:17*. Harare: Government Printer.

—— (1998). *Regional, Town and Country Planning Act, Chapter 29:12*. Harare: Government Printer.

—— (1996). *Mines and Mineral Act, Chapter 21:05*. Harare: Government Printer.

Kampala Convention (2009): *African Union Convention for the Protection and Assistance of Internally Displaced Persons in Africa*. African Union.

ODI (1999). *Human Settlements and their Place in Development*. London: Overseas Development Institute.

Parr J. B., (1999). "Growth-pole Strategies in Regional Economic Planning. A Retrospective View. Part 1. Origins and Advocacy", *Urban Studies*, 36(7), pp.195-215

Rukuni, M. (1994). *Report of the Commission of Inquiry into Appropriate Agricultural Land Tenure Systems*. Harare: Government Printers.

Sachikonye, L. (2005). "The Land is the Economy", *African Security Review*, 14(3), pp. 31-44.

Utete, C. M. B. (2003). *Report of the Presidential Land Review Committee on the Implementation of the Fast Track Land Reform Programme, 2000-2002*. Harare: Government Printer.

ZHRNGOF (2010). *Land Reform and Property Rights in Zimbabwe*. Harare: Zimbabwe Human Rights NGO Forum.

3

Land Tenure Systems, Neoliberal Policies and Displacement in Zimbabwe: An Overview

Steve Mberi

1. Introduction

This chapter provides a general survey of Zimbabwean experiences on a continuum of land tenure regimes, particularly focusing on rural communities within statutory land tenure regimes, with the intention of illuminating the challenges regarding the security of the communities from dispossession and how land tenure security can be improved to avert unjustified evictions. The study examines the country's waves of land tenure reforms before, during and after the Fast Track Land Reform Programme (FTLRP) in the 2000s, the differentiated practices of land alienation, and the dispossession of the agrarian communities by different elements (state and non-state actors, formal and informal), as well as the substantial destruction of the means of production of the peasantry.

To have a better clarification of the logic underlying land titling, the chapter first conceptualises the land dispossessions by providing an overview of the Zimbabwean experiences in a multi-form land tenure system. It further goes on to explain and classify the concept of tenure and the tenurial regimes operative in Zimbabwe. Going further, in explaining Zimbabwe's land tenurial system, the chapter also raises the problems and issues associated with it in relation to all the constituent elements of tenure, including allocation of land or land rights, security of those rights, land acquisition, dispossession, and compensation. Subsequently, the chapter discusses the challenges of land tenure security and the eminent dispossessions that are eroding the livelihoods of the peasantry in Chiadzwa and Chisumbanje.

In light of the findings, the chapter then examines a range of alternative policy measures aimed at improving and enhancing the tenure security among the peasantry in Zimbabwe. This entails discussing the rationale of enhancing the land administration system and consolidation of land laws and related regulations towards improving the coherence of the institutions that deal with customary tenure. Furthermore, the chapter examines the differentiated impacts of dispossessions from a gender perspective and how women remain a vulnerable group on land rights.

2. Conceptual framework

The adoption of the Western neoliberal policies and prescriptions that support privatisation and marketisation as sole paths for development has created the crisis faced by the peasants in Zimbabwe and elsewhere in the developing world. Neo-colonial and internal colonial perspectives and analytics were used to critically examine the dispossession of the rural communities which is inspired by the neoliberal orthodox. Problems of forced relocations, evictions, forced assimilation of peasants into global markets has been brought forward by the project of development (Fisher 1999; Kapoor 2012). Processes of dispossession, evictions, displacements or market integration have been augmented by the post-'Economic Structural Adjustment Programmes' (ESAPs) era and also by the second republic through the new dispensation formed in 2017 with the quest for investment through engaging global capital, most of which follows a Eurocentric model of development. The neoliberal policies by the Breton Woods institutions to achieve development were introduced in Zimbabwe in the 1990s through the adoption of ESAPs. Like any other developing country that adopted ESAPs, Zimbabwe was showing signs of a debt crisis and increasing poverty, which saw the peasants' and workers' conditions of social reproduction deteriorate (Moyo and Yeros 2005a), leading to the state as the political entity organising internal imperialist and capitalist policies that benefited the elite mostly (Hwami, Madzanire and Hwami 2018).

Since the year 2000, when the country embarked on the radical Fast Track Land Reform Programme (FTLRP), it was faced with punitive sanctions and isolation by the Western countries, particularly the UK and the USA (Raftopoulos 2006, Hwami 2010), which led to the state invoking different strategies to proclaim its economic and political interests. Based on the need to revive the economy bled by sanctions and international isolation, the Zimbabwean government initiated the 'Look East'-policy with the state establishing ties with Chinese capital to venture into lucrative operations in various projects in infrastructure development and mining (Hwami et al. 2018). This affected rural communities who faced evictions in areas where there was potential of resources, such as diamonds in Chiadzwa. In some instances, there was use of force through state power to silence the vulnerable communities who resisted the capitalist system that was imposed on them. The lack of tenure security by rural communities, and also the issue of eminent domain of the state, places landholders in a position that is vulnerable to evictions, with or without compensation. This concurs with notions by Harvey (2003) that monopoly violence by the state together with definitions of legality plays a critical role in promoting marketisation and privatisation policies.

The evictions and relocations of rural communities in various parts of Zimbabwe show how capitalist development works. Neoliberalism, which involves the transfer of productive assets from the state to private entities, drives modern development. Land, minerals and other natural resources formulate productive assets. The development driven by neoliberal forces involves the dissipation of local livelihoods, cultures, social structures, and traditional ways of life. The idea of 'development' within this context becomes questionable, particularly for rural communities affected by evictions in areas such as Chiadzwa and Chisumbanje, or elsewhere where people are not being lifted out of poverty but made more vulnerable through takeover of their lands. It thus cannot be over-emphasised that land is a critical productive asset for Zimbabwe as an agro-based economy, where agriculture is the second highest export earner after mining (see Chambati, Mazwi and Mberi 2016). Hence the alleged sense of enhancing the lives of people has transformed the meaning of 'development' to mean displacement of rural communities, as capitalist tendencies continue to disrupt sources of livelihoods that rural communities traditionally relied on.

The evictions and relocations of the rural communities confirm a defeat of their indigenous knowledge systems being overtaken by foreign knowledge systems that ignored cultural beliefs, devastated sustainable livelihoods and considered rural communities as objects for resource exploitation (Hwami et al. 2018). The resistance by the communities to be evicted for cultural reasons is viewed as anti-progress against development.

The current form of accumulation by dispossession, as evidenced in the rural communities of Chiadzwa and Chisumbanje, presents a process whereby other peoples are dominated with their destinies being shaped according to Western customs and prescriptions of seeing and perceiving the world (Tucker 1999). The once autonomous rural communities have been proletarianised and turned into cheap labour providers in the mining companies, while others are left out without employment in order to create a labour reserve. This concurs with observations by Chambati, Mazwi and Mberi (2018) on exploitative relations, where peasant farmers dispossessed of their means of production are reduced to employees who survive on a monthly wage on or off the farm. Such arrangements barricade accumulation from below by the rural communities, while upholding and entrenching agrarian accumulation by capital, both local and foreign.

3. Brief history and structure of Zimbabwe's agrarian landscape

3.1. Land tenure: a synopsis

Shivji et al. (1998) define land tenure as the legal rules recognised and applied in any given country for the allocation or acquisition of land rights, the practical content of those rights, their protection in law, their disposal and or extinction, as well as their regulation. This means a land tenurial system involves the process of how and by whom the land rights are acquired, how they are regulated, protected and disposed of or estranged. The rights and obligations a person is entitled to regarding land, its products or anything attached to it as against the state and others relates to the incidents of land tenure. In summary, a tenurial system is fundamentally established by or of a package of rights and obligations a person has to acquire or be allocated to occupy, hold and use land and all its products subject to the guidelines, rules, procedures, and limits the state may execute in relation to land use, conservation, planning, disposal, and transfer. To this end, complications of land tenure revolve around issues of access to and acquisition of land rights. The most critical aspects of any tenurial regime is the security of tenure or landholdings among individuals or landholders.

3.2. The emergence of received and customary tenure regimes

The colonial settlers in Zimbabwe came with their law, received as the Roman-Dutch/English common law system, and created a legal regime of ownership that positioned them well in terms of protection by awarding them the largest bundle of rights known as the received law regimes (see Shivji et al. 1998). This was the emergence of the freehold and leasehold tenure system with the settlers' land in 'Large-Scale Commercial Farms' (LSCF) held on freehold, a tenurial system considered to award total ownership held in perpetuity with enormous rights in terms of ownership, control, manage, use, and disposal of property (ibid.). The two systems, freehold and leaseholds, became almost undistinguishable in terms of large-scale farming and ownership. These tenurial regimes, underpinned by racial segregation, were simulated in urban areas to define white and black residence and commercial activities. Given the amount of protection the freehold tenure received from the state and its associated institutions in terms of the received law, it was presented as the most secure form of tenure.

The black indigenes or natives in the reserves were on the other hand granted occupation rights of the land through state permission as the ultimate owner or the holder of radical title (Shivji et al. 1998). Criminal law and sanctions controlled their occupation and use of land with no legally rooted rights as against the state or those under freehold or leasehold title. The natives were allowed to continue relating to each other under customary law, a system that also administered their tenures and land relations. But their permission to occupy and use land could be withdrawn by administrative sanction, including through forced evictions, at the will of the state with the lands being appropriated without resorting to the law. This apparently made customary law tenure to be presented and perceived as an insecure and fragile form of tenure.

Furthermore, inequalities and inequities were also embedded within the weak and fragile customary land rights, despite the shadow constructed colonial power structures and struggles which blindly placed communities under customary law as harmonious and homogenous. In actual fact, there was a differentiation that emerged along social and gender lines that resulted in unequal and inequitable land access and use, especially in terms of the female gender. This led to an obvious manifestation of discriminatory ownership and inheritance rubrics prejudiced against wives, widows and daughters.

An asymmetry was therefore created and sanctified between received and customary law tenure systems with a hierarchical, unequal dualism placing received laws tenure as more secure and superior in all facets, law, practice, and perception. Customary tenure, unprotected by law, was considered insecure and presented and perceived as primitive and not suitable to attract investment and development, which further accentuated female gender inequities.

3.3. Overview of Zimbabwean land tenure systems and characteristics

As discussed in the previous section, Zimbabwe is characterised by a bimodal land tenure system which was inherited from the colonial regime and maintained as such until now (see figure 1). This system consists of the customary land tenure regime and statutory received tenure regime, where various landholders and/or land-users can be located within this land tenure regime. The 'Communal Areas', legally called customary areas were created during the colonial period as 'Tribal Trust Lands' to accommodate the indigenous black people dispossessed of their pieces of land by the colonial European settlers (Arrighi 1970; Palmer 1977). The colonial authorities then converted the land alienated from the indigenes to received laws (freehold, leaseholds, state permit) (Moyo 2009).

Figure 1: Bi-modal tenure regime. Source: Moyo (2009)

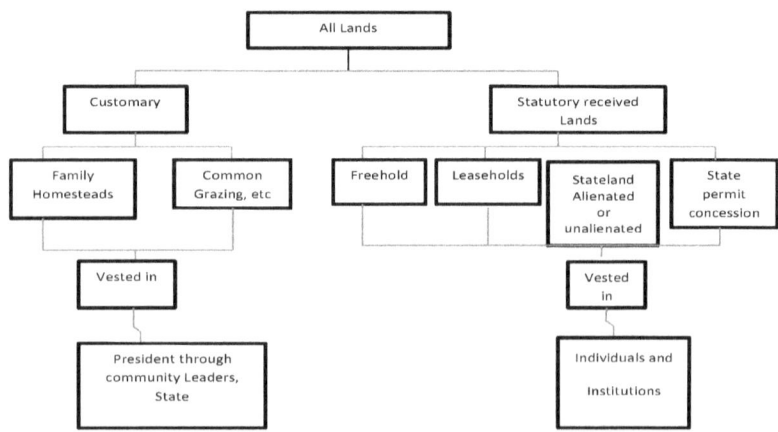

3.3.1. Freehold tenure

Freehold tenure is a system based on individual ownership of land held by an individual or institution under and in terms of a title deed in permanence. This system is also referred to as freehold title. This system historically involved total rights of ownership with the utmost bundle of rights which can be held by an individual over land. Apart from being the indication of ownership and title, the title deed is the instrument of conveyance or transference of the land from one person to another which takes place in terms of the Deeds Registries Act [Chapter 20:05]. The title deed is decisive and ultimate proof of ownership and that ownership is guaranteed by the state. Under this tenure regime, ownership of land can only pass from one person to another by way of a deed of transfer, known as the title deed, which is prepared by a conveyancer and executed by the Registrar of Deeds. It is in this context that the security of freehold is understood as a certainty and incontestability of title as supported by the title deed. The liberty to pass on this title to a purchaser or some other person evidently highlights the security of the owner and is also said to ensure open and fluent property and land markets.

Although historically, the freehold system is a flawed tenure system closely linked to colonial land appropriation and concentration of land ownership, it is still regarded in Zimbabwe as a more secure and internally intelligible tenure system. Nonetheless, due to the state's wide-ranging acquisitive powers under the provisions of the Land Acquisition Act [Chapter 20:10], freehold individual tenure is not that secure as against the state (see Shivji et al. 1998). However, the state is legally prohibited from interfering with and abrogating freehold land rights without fair compensation which protects the land owners against arbitrary evictions.

3.3.2. Leasehold tenure

Leasehold tenure system is a contemporary and flexible tenure system compared to freehold tenure, as it permits the state more flexibility to distribute land in terms of lease agreements, which may be long or short leases. In regard to security, long leases of 99 years can be as secure as is freehold tenure. The principle of leasehold tenure is that land belonging to one person, either as an individual, institution or the state, is leased to another person by a contractual agreement and the lease agreement then registered against the title of that land to create real rights enforceable against the whole world (see Shivji et al. 1998). In Zimbabwe leases are registrable in terms of section 65 of the Deeds Registries Act and any land held by the state or an individual under a title deed or land which has been surveyed and a diagram for it drawn and approved in terms of the Land Survey Act [Chapter 20:12] is eligible for leasing to anyone by agreement. The leasing of state land is regulated by the Agricultural Land Settlement Act [Chapter 20:01] and the Rural Land Act [Chapter 20:18]. State land leased in terms of and under these statutes can be leased either on a lease to buy basis or on a closed lease with no option to buy. Currently, the Government of Zimbabwe has been offering two types of leases, 25 and 99 year leases, to beneficiaries of the land reform programme who received A2 commercial farms, although many are yet to get these leases (see SMAIAS forthcoming).

3.3.3. Permit tenure

The permit tenure regime functions through the issuance of permits by the state for land occupation by individuals. The occupation and use rights of the individual occupants are completely administered by and reliant on the terms of the enabling permit. Resettlement lands designated for small-scale farms, including under the Fast Track Land Reform Programme, have been allocated to and occupied by settlers under a permit tenurial regime supposedly authorised by section 6 of the Rural Land Act which permits the Minister of Agriculture and Lands to "lease, sell or otherwise dispose of state land for such purposes and subject to such conditions as he may determine". Acting in terms of section 6 of the Rural Land Act, the incumbent minister allocates resettlement land under a permit system in terms of which the state retains full title and ownership of the land while granting the inhabitants occupation and use rights over that land. The origin of the permit system is not statutory, but administrative in that the entire permit system is not specifically provided for in statutes and regulations but arises from administrative discretion and policy.

    The absence of a precise legal regulatory framework for the permit system means that both, the criteria for allocating resettlement land and settler selection together with the terms of those allocations, become matters of discretion, which leaves the system open to administrative abuse, patronage and corruption, thereby compromising certainty, predictability and transparency. This obviously results in tenure insecurity since the land rights of all settlers in the resettlement areas are not defined and regulated by any statute or regulations, but rather determined administratively by

Sector	Tenure type	1980		2000		2010	
		Farms/hh	Ha (ha)	Farms/hh	Ha (ha)	Farms/hh	Ha (ha)
Communal Area	Customary	700,000	16,400,000	1,050,000	16,400,000	1,100,000	16,400,000
A1	Permit					146,000	4,137,000
Old Resettlement	Permit			75,000	3,667,000	75,000	3,667,000
Small-scale commercial	Leasehold	8,500	1,400,000	8500	1,400,000	8,500	1,400,000
A2	Leasehold			4,700		22,900	3,508,900
Large-Scale Commercial	Freehold/Lease	5,400	13,000,000	4,700	8,691,600	1,154	648,000
State	Freehold/Lease		500,000		721,000		721,000
Urban land	Public/Freehold Lease		196,000		250,000		250,000
Forest/parks	State owned/Lease		5,074,000		5,074,000		5,074,000
Unallocated land							
Total[1]		713,900	36,570,000	1,138,200	36,203,600	1,353,554	35,805,900

Table 1: Land distribution by tenure category. Source: Compiled by SMAIAS from Moyo (2011); Moyo and Yeros (2005).

[1] Total hectarages do not tally due to rounding off; some agricultural land is now residential (urban).

the responsible minister who, entirely at his discretion, sets the terms and conditions of settlement through a regime not set by law but by administrative sanction (Shivji et al. 1998). Hence the permit system represents a poor form of rightlessness by occupants and users of land in Zimbabwe which render the occupants under this regime vulnerable to evictions without adequate legal protection for compensation.

3.3.4. Customary tenure

Customary land also referred to as 'Communal Areas' can be tracked down to the colonial era in which it was known as 'Native Reserves' and established randomly in the dry marginal zones of the country to accommodate black indigenes dispossessed of their prime land by the colonialists (Palmer 1977; Rukuni 1994). This displaced peasantry was provided land for residency, cropping and grazing livestock. As the development of European agriculture intensified, African peasants were forcibly moved to these areas gradually (Arrighi 1970). In 1965, the native reserves were renamed to 'Tribal Trust Lands' (TTLs) and to 'Communal Areas' in 1981 post-independence (Rukuni 1994). Customary areas are home to about 1,100,000 households in Zimbabwe (Moyo 2011a: 512) with families in these areas accessing an average of between 0.2 and 5.0 hectares arable hectares and shared grazing land (Moyo 2011a: 512), but over 70% arable land are less than 2.5 hectares in size (Moyo 1995: 157).

In this tenure regime land is administered through several acts such as the Communal Land Act, Traditional Leaders Act and Rural District Councils Act. Traditional authorities under the leadership of the chiefs are the most protuberant land administrators at the local level. Although the Rural District Councils (RDC) have a legal ultimate responsibility to administer the customary lands, traditional leaders continue to be considered as the custodians of these lands. The chiefs, headmen *(sadunhu)* and village heads *(sabhuku)* compose the traditional authority. Within the RDC, elected ward representatives (councillors) and the chief executive responsible for daily council operations compose the RDC. Traditional chiefs are ex officio members of the RDC, while headmen and village heads are in the Ward Development Committees (WADCO) and Village Development Committees (VIDCO), respectively.

The Communal Land Act concentrates power and authority on state structures granting unjustified rights to individual landholders. In terms of documentation to prove ownership, there are no documents to prove rights to land in the customary areas. Nonetheless, there are registers of households which are maintained at the village level and indicate allocation, occupation and use of land in line with customary law. Furthermore, the documentation used for payments of levies and taxes to the RDCs also serves as proof of lawful land occupation (Chambati and Mazwi 2020). A study by Mazwi et al. (2017) exposed that communal area households need to produce a letter from the village head or local agricultural extension officer to prove for land occupation to access various agricultural services.

4. Study methodology

This study employed a qualitative approach to illuminate Zimbabwe's land tenure systems and the impact of land evictions of various communities across the tenure regimes, but with more focus on the rural communities in various districts of the country. Secondary literature was used to explore how tenure insecurity exposes communities to dispossessions that arise from a myriad of factors, but with developmental projects being the main focus. Data from the SMAIAS 2013/14 baseline survey, which covered six districts of the country (Chipinge, Chiredzi, Goromonzi, Kwekwe, Mangwe and Zvimba), was also relied on. Interviews were also done with participants from Chisumbanje and Chiadzwa, with some interviews conducted in 2019 and follow up interviews with key personnel carried out in April 2020. Due to the COVID-19 pandemic and government lockdown restrictions, these were carried out telephonically. These include interviews with the traditional leaders, government officials and the Platform for Youth Development (PYD) representative. Traditional leaders were critical in this study because of the role they play in the rural communities as custodians of the various aspects of life of the communities. The participants interviewed were purposefully sampled (see Neutens and Rubinson 2002, p.125). Gathered data was analysed and synced with the secondary sources to inform the discussion of the issues raised.

5. Challenges to land tenure security for rural community landholders

This section examines the forms of land tenure security obtaining across all the tenure regimes, including the newly resettled areas under received laws, but with particular focus on the communal areas under customary tenure. A further examination on land dispossessions and/or evictions is carried out and the nature of land conflicts currently being experienced is explored to deduce the tenure security of landholders. This section mainly focuses on the rural communities within the communal areas, however, with a few inferences across other tenure regimes.

Development-induced displacements (DIDs) through projects, such as dams, roads, growth points, as well as foreign direct investments (FDIs) in mining and agriculture, also pose major threats to the tenure security of customary areas as communities are dispossessed of their land by the state in the public interest, in many circumstances without compensation (see table 2). Some dispossessions to note include the displacement of an estimated 4,321 households in Marange customary areas to create way for diamond mining by domestic and foreign capital in 2013 (see Chambati and Mazwi 2020; Mberi and Mazwi forthcoming). Preceding that, a similar tragedy occurred in Chipinge District in 2010, where 1,800 households were dispossessed to pave way for an ethanol project (Moyo 2011b).

Despite the belief of insecurity within the customary areas, a survey by SMAIAS in 2013/14 found that the customary area households were seemingly secure against evictions and/or threats of the same, compared to the A1 and A2 households. The survey found only 1.6 percent of the surveyed landholders faced eviction threats. The same study also exposed the vulnerability of women to losing land after a change in their marital status on account of the operation of customary laws that marginalise women's rights, as discussed in depth in section six.

Persistence of land conflicts and threats of evictions or actual evictions reflect the failure of the existing tenure systems to protect rural communities on their land. The land rights in communal areas are allocated to families for arable and residential land, while they share grazing land and other common land, such as forests and mountains, with the village community. Family rights are generally held in trust mostly by male heads of family, who in turn customarily safeguards access to all adult and married family members, including women, through an inclusive and participatory decision-making process (Rukuni and Matondi 2014). This traditional administration which warranted land tenure security at a higher level is now corrupted and the capacities weakened which also explains the unfortunate tagging of customary systems as gender biased which, however, is a contemporary characteristic. It is unfortunate that there have not been any efforts by the colonial or the post-independence governments to seriously invest in understanding the customary systems

Table 2: Land administration issues in communal lands.
Source: Rukuni and Matondi (2014)[2]

Who	Process	Issues
President MLGPWNH RDC TL	Through the CLA the President, MLGPWNH, RDC, and TL have administrative rights over communal areas. Ownership of communal areas is in the presidents jurisdiction RDC allocated land to the people through its traditional leaders (chiefs, *sadunhu, sabhuku*) RDC with the approval of MLGPWNH issues permits to use the land of communal areas for purposes other than residential and arable. MLGPWNH in consultation with the RDC can set aside land for the establishment of townships, business centre, irrigation schemes, and other developmental activities	There is no clear definition of the management structure of the roles of TLs, councillors, district administrators, and district land officers Though still participating in land administration issues, the legal framework has removed all administrative powers from traditional institutions. This has created space for land allocation disputes between traditional and RDC institutions. Cultural norms and values are not gender-sensitive and women have no clear land rights as well as land inheritance rights. There are no survey diagrams an individual can use to identify their land allocation and be able to also use them as collateral. Customary and permit tenure policies have alienated landholders from the benefits of land market developments in communal and resettlement areas. The expected gains have accrued to the state organs and bypassed landholders, because the state expropriates land rights from these landholders whenever investment opportunities arise. Recent cases include the Marange diamonds investments whose diamond income now accrues to the state, despite being located in the Marange/Chiadzwa communal areas.

2 CLA=Communal Land Act; CLLC=Customary Law and Local Courts Act; MLGPWNH=Ministry of Local Governance, Public Works and National Housing; MLAWCRR=Ministry of Lands, Agriculture, Water, Climate and Rural Resettlement; RDC=Rural District Council; TL=Traditional leaders; TLA=Traditional Leaders Act; LAS=Land administration system, LIMS=Land information management system.

Who	Process	Issues
TL	Through the TLA and CLLCA, traditional leaders lead dispute resolution in civil cases. There are local courts under the customary law which are presided over by headmen and chiefs.	However local courts have no jurisdiction in cases involving disputes over land. The common/statute laws have superseded the customary legal framework. Accordingly, statutory bodies (RDCs, MLGPWNH and the president) are now empowered to administer customary lands which would otherwise be managed by customary institutions. The CLA denies land ownership rights to communities and does not offer freehold or leaseholds to communities, individuals or RDCs. This undermines the bargaining strength of communities in the event of land disputes between communities or between communities and state.
MLAWCRR MLGPWNH	Land information management on state land is therefore fragmented between MLGPWNH and MLAWCRR.	No information on various land administration processes. Poor coordination of LAS information holders. Limited public and user access to LIMS.
MLAWCRR Private Investors	The role of the MLAWCRR in the customary tenure areas has so far been limited to a few site specific demands for survey, pegging, valuation, and titling.	The CLA allocates land rights at community level and yet no compensation is given in the event a community loses part of its land rights. Compensation is however paid to households displaced to create space for a state activity. Land transfers that reduce the quantity of community rights over commonly held areas are not being compensated for, in spite of the fact that land is transferred in favour of profitable enterprises like hotels or mineral operations.

and modernising them on traditional principles of inclusion, equity and consultative process (ibid.).

5.1. Land struggles of rural communities

Rural District Councils have the formal legal mandate to allocate land use rights in the communal areas, but unfortunately in practice diverse authorities including village heads, headmen, chiefs, ruling party village chairpersons, and VIDCO chairpersons are all involved in the allocation of land. This has created a de facto conflict in the allocation of land between the traditional leaders and local government structures, although formal legal authority rests with the RDCs. This has created confusion, uncertainty and corruption. Furthermore, the system is seriously biased against women (see Gaidzanwa 2011) at both community and household levels. The subdivision and consolidation of land parcels in communal areas to accommodate other uses, in particular investments in mining, agriculture and tourism, is mostly influenced by traditional leaders. A case in point is in Chiadzwa where traditional leaders, particularly the chief, played a significant role to allow for the relocation of the communities paving way for the diamond operations, as evidenced by an alleged lucrative compensation package awarded to him by a diamond company, according to an interview with a village head.

The Chisumbanje contestation marks another struggle between villagers and local capital over communal land, influenced by the state machinery. Although the traditional leaders have a mandate of allocating land, their authority to halt evictions and dispossessions accumulating from above becomes minimal and in some cases is of no influence. The established green fuel estate in Chisumbanje, owned by the local bourgeois Billy Rautenbach, has been a major case in point. The project has been encroaching onto the communities' land and decimating the peasantry's only means of production they have been relying on for many years. In a myriad of cases, boundary issues have emerged between the green fuel capital project and the peasantry, with the former accused by the latter of encroaching on their land and dispossessing them, resulting in the villagers and traditional leaders protesting and threatening to take legal action. To quote verbatim of one affected villager:

> I have been living on this land since l was a kid, I am now 36 years, and l don't know of any place to call home besides here.

> We were raised and schooled here, doing our farming on the very land in question, and all of a sudden we faced eviction because of interests of a company which promised development through the creation of employment for the communities, which never yielded any result because not many locals benefitted and were absorbed by the project. Although we were allocated alternative land here in Transau, it was too small, only half a hectare, with poor quality soils. Moreover, it is very far, over 10 km, from my home. It's a pity for us, we are living in more poverty than before.

A key interview with a local councillor also highlighted that, despite the commitment by the Government of Zimbabwe in 2010 to compensate the displaced villagers affected by the green fuel project, to date no meaningful progress has been achieved, which caused land disputes to be an endless phenomenon.

The Chiadzwa case presents yet another sad story within the spectres of the local communities. The discovery of the precious mineral (diamonds) in the Chiadzwa area brought excitement to the state through the envisaged development, but on the other side mal-development and disaster emerged for the Chiadzwa communities, who faced abrupt dispossessions of their means of production. A number of strategies were engaged to dispossess and relocate the Chiadzwa people from their traditional lands to pave way for diamond mining by the state and international capital. Most accounts relate to the brutal force being employed by the police and military to thwart illegal mining activities perpetrated by the people from outside Chiadzwa, while the local people were also caught in cross-fire as they were also involved in the illegal mining activities. According to Chingano et al. (2015), the militant response by the government was meant to displace and relocate the Chiadzwa people through victimising the local people who live in the areas surrounding the diamond fields, a process they conceptualised as "militarized capitalism".

Within the media, the discovery of diamonds was presented as national development and better prospects for Zimbabweans to counter the crisis imposed by the Western countries through sanctions. Employment creation was guaranteed by the state and expected through the mining operations that would formally operate. But this, according to the displaced, never materialised. Another villager bemoaned:

> The Chinese companies hardly employ people from here. All their

operations are highly mechanised, there is nothing left for us and we are starving. The discovery of diamonds in our area should have been a blessing not a curse.

Local traditional leaders were given the task of explaining and convincing their people of the rationale for displacements and relocation, which also came with a token being awarded to them to silence them against standing against the government supported development project (see Hwami, Madzamire and Hwami 2018). To quote one displaced villager from Chiadzwa:

> We thought the traditional leaders would stand for us against the displacements, but they were against us their people, and decided to stand with the foreigners and the state, simply because they had personal benefits awarded to them.

This entails that the role of traditional leaders to protect their communities against evictions was compromised.

5.2. *Compensation and valuation*

However, there are some cases where communities affected by development programmes have been compensated. Nonetheless, the area of contention in most cases is valuation of properties with no evidence of independent valuators being used by the state to assess levels of compensation. Furthermore, there are some evictions that are not even compensated, which in many instances brought conflicts and disputes between the state and the communities facing eviction, and resulted in resistance through various ways by the latter. A recent case is the Mutare High Court ruling presided by Justice Mwayera on 24 July 2020 which granted an order to stop the eviction of 750 households in Munyokowere village, Chipinge District, Manicaland Province. The order stopped the intended demolition of occupied or unoccupied structures that belong to the villagers, after the authorities threatened to demolish the structures of the villagers. The reason for the eviction note was that the communities are allegedly occupying the gazetted land without lawful authority, despite having been legitimately allocated the area by the Ministry of Local Government, Public Works and National Housing in 1992 (see Dhliwayo and Joala 2020).

Another case is in Chiadzwa, Manicaland Province where companies were tasked to compensate the affected communities who lost their land and homes to pave way for the diamond mining. Land for resettlement was provided for free by the state, although there were contentious issues regarding arability. The companies were supposed to provide housing and services to the resettled families, which consisted of modest support of food hampers, fertilizer and seeds only provided during the first days. Hwami, Madzamire and Hwami (2018) also report that 300 families displaced by a Chinese diamond company called Anjin from the Chirasika area of Chiadzwa to Arda Transau in Odzi were compensated with three-roomed houses. Another study showed that 474 families were relocated by Anjin and were paid USD $1,000 as compensation, which they resisted citing the wealth they lost was beyond this value.[2]

According to a study by Konyana and Sipeyiye (2015), the state through the Agricultural and Rural Development Authority (ARDA) claimed the local communities of Chisumbanje were aware of the green fuel project's establishment and were adequately warned before against erecting any permanent structures and planting crops in the area, as it was approved for the ethanol project. The state thus remains obstinate that some evictions did not deserve any compensation as the villagers were forewarned (Mberi and Mazwi forthcoming). The villagers nonetheless justify their occupation on the land citing the late onset of the project, which took far too long to commence. This led to fierce clashes between the villagers and the investors due to the villagers contesting against the evictions. It is critical to note that the villagers also claimed ancestral links on the pieces of land they were being evicted from, a claim difficult to ignore. Ancestral link claims to land are common elsewhere and also in Zimbabwe, as clearly demonstrated by studies in Zimbabwe post FTLRP that demand for land during the FTLRP was partly driven by ancestry and historical links (see Moyo et al. 2009; Scoones et al. 2010).

In terms of internal land reallocations, there is evidence that such reallocations that happen in most communal areas through traditional leaders hardly provide for compensation. A key approach used, is one of negotiation with the families and deals are usually struck in the case of internal reallocation. However, there have been reported cases of land sales in communal areas, particularly of grazing land by chiefs and other traditional leaders, which at law is regarded as illegal. It would appear that there is no reference authority when it comes to functions of valuation and compensation in communal areas, but rather an *ad hoc* approach

---

2 "Diamonds Fail to Sparkle at Chiadzwa (by P. Muzulu and W. Zhangazha)", *The Zimbabwe Independent*, 23 June 2011.

administered by the public or private entity that is acquiring land from current users (see table 3).

6. Gender relations in land tenure

This section gives a critical account on the challenges being faced by women across all tenure regimes, particularly in the newly established A1 and A2, which is very critical in triangulating the dynamics of land tenure beyond a monolithic tenure regime perspective.

Although there have been significant strides regarding gender relations in other spheres, gender relations within the land tenure, which involves oppressive customary and policy based patriarchal relations, remains unequal with inequitable land rights still applying particularly to vulnerable women, such as the divorcees, aged, as well as to married women, especially in polygamous relations (see Moyo 2009; Chingarande 2007). However, through the gazetting of Statutory Instrument 53 of 2014, the government strives to enhance the security of women on land within marriage through the provision of joint spouse ownership registration of agricultural land on the A1 permit, which entails the loosening of power by men to legally dispose of the land use right without the consent of their spouses (see Mazwi et al. 2018).

There is varied empirical evidence on women's access to redistributed land in their own right, with government sources indicating that about 17% of the land beneficiaries were women (Utete 2003; Buka 2002). SMAIAS sample survey (2013/14) claims the proportion of women who received FTLRP land in their own right was around 20.5%, with more women benefitting in the A1 sector (23.5%) compared to the A2 sector (16.2%). Other studies claim women constitute between 10% and 28% of the beneficiaries (see Chingarande 2006; Utete 2003). The effectiveness of such land access, regarding control of the benefits, still needs to be adequately illuminated by research. Actual evictions or threats of evictions were reported by about 12% of beneficiaries (AIAS Baseline Survey 2007; SMAIAS Survey 2013/14), which is proportionately higher given that fewer women benefited in their individual right from the land reform.

The fundamental sources of gender differentiation on land tenure inequity mainly point to the constraints faced by women in applying for land, which include gender biases among the selecting structures which comprise mainly men, as well as bureaucratic constraints, inadequate

Table 3: Current status of customary land rights in communal areas.

Source: Rukuni and Matondi (2014)

Analysis of rights	Type of expected rights	What is working	Current challenges	Effects	Scope for reform
Use rights	Rights to grow crops, trees on residential and cropping land, to make permanent improvements on homestead, graze livestock and harvest trees and fruits under community regulation	Freedom of use of land (residency, field and grazing)	Underinvestment; land pressures; land and environmental degradation; escalating land conflicts	Reduced investment in communal areas	Strengthening land governance at community level
Land transfer rights	Rights to sell, give, mortgage, lease, rent or bequeath	Distress land sales do not happen; communal land is not transferable.	Illegal land transfers; unplanned commercialisation of peri-urban land	Financial institutions not interested in vesting capital in sector; increasing land conflicts	Pressure for formalisation, allowing for valuation and compensation through community and local government suctioned systems

Analysis of rights	Type of expected rights	What is working	Current challenges	Effects	Scope for reform
Exclusion and inclusion rights	Rights to exclude and/or include to effect use and transfers, and to be able to make independent decisions on the piece of land	Rights to use are guaranteed and families can make arrangements for inheritance	Problems of inheritance starting to emerge especially in peri-urban located communal lands	Inability to deal with invaders in peri-urban areas	Defining the markers of village boundaries in a participatory manner
Enforcement rights	Rights to the legal, judicial, institutional and administrative provisions to guarantee use, transfer and exclusion rights	Traditional leaders effective in land management and organizing people; internal reallocations are hardly contested	Traditional leaders accused of selling land illegally when faced with increasing populations; village heads have opened up new residential and arable lands, in the process squeezing out grazing and risking environmental degradation; land governance structures decaying	Traditional leaders who sell land are compromised and cannot enforce exclusion; plus poor records; some communal and old resettlement land regressing into "open access" land with no effective governance, regulation and policing	Improvements in adjudication, administering mutation, record-keeping; increase capacity for handling land conflicts

information on the process, and weak mobilisation by women's activist organisations for applications (Moyo 2009).

There is also weak empirical evidence regarding land tenures on which land access is provided to households, rather than individual applicants, and its gender equity. However, SMAIAS (2013/14) study exposed that the majority of the "offer letters" (in A2 schemes) and A1 permit allocations issued were given in the names of the male spouses. Interviews with key government officials exposed reports of reversals with some women, who had been given tenure documents as individuals in their own rights, going back to government officials seeking re-issuance of the tenure documents in the husbands' name, even though the Government of Zimbabwe policy is to offer spouses joint tenure. This perpetuates the vulnerability to dispossession among women, especially in the case of polygamous marriages, death of the male spouse or even state-induced displacements.

Conflicts and evictions and/or threats of dispossession faced by women from various sources are a major constraint on their tenure security on land gained through the FTLRP. According to SMAIAS Survey (2013/14), A2 women landholders were more vulnerable to land conflicts as reported by 34% of them, in comparison to 10.8% in the A1 sector. The most common source of land disputes are boundary disputes with neighbours across all the tenure regimes under received and customary tenures. The survey also found that there were more women landholders who faced eviction threats from their land, particularly in the A2 sector, as indicated by 14.6% compared to 3.2% amongst male land owners. Various sources of eviction threats for female landholders in the A2 areas were noted, coming mainly from neighbours, war veterans and former white commercial farmers. Although women have advanced socially and economically in acquiring land, their vulnerability to intimidation and displacement exacerbates due to socially constructed roles and relations within a patriarchal society (Bedi and Cea 2017).

Furthermore, the customary law's recognition of the male head of the household as holder of land impedes the holding of primary land rights by women. This relegates women to holding secondary rights resulting from and negotiated through the husband (see Gaidzanwa 2011). This obliterates the bargaining power by women to negotiate land access and contest against land evictions. Myriad features of customary law and practices trigger the discrimination against land access and asset accumulation by women, as well as a variety of drawbacks which women face owing to their institutionalised insecurity in marriages and over divorces (see Moyo 2009). These include disparities over land inheritance, the sharing of property upon divorce, and the male head of household's control over resources, such as commodity sales, income, cattle, etc. (ibid.).

The protection of women against evictions is also hindered and limited by the preponderance of men in decision-making within the land administration structures. Save for the Zimbabwe Land Commission (ZLC), which has more women representation, most state land institutions have a pervasive influence of patriarchy within their functionaries across all levels, with women constituting less than 10% of employees in positions of influence (Moyo 2009). Furthermore, there has been limited capacity of vibrant women's organisations to mobilise for redress and enhance the protection of women within the patriarchal power relations of society, which negatively affects the overall gender balancing of tenure rights (see Moyo 2009).

The insecurity associated with eviction or loss of livelihoods and resources summarises the challenges which women and their families face as they are dispossessed from their community and resources. Urban and transient poor, a myriad who live in make-shift settlements at road sides, have been turned a blind eye to. An example can be drawn from Mazowe, where over three years have passed with evicted families, many of which are women and children, living on the side of the road.

7. Aborting unjustified displacements: way forward

7.1. Enhancing the 'Land Administration System' (LAS) in Zimbabwe

To avert the arbitrary evictions and strengthen the land rights of communities, the greatest task by the Government of Zimbabwe is to come up with a coherent and well-functioning LAS, which is resourced and works with a coordinated system across all the land tenure regimes.[3] However, the major challenge lies also in the quest to enhance the capacity and coordinating role of the Ministry of Lands, Agriculture, Water, Climate and Rural Resettlement, while also consolidating the Zimbabwe Land Commission (ZLC) to "ensure accountability, fairness and transparency

---

3 See "Towards a National Gender-sensitive Land Policy: The Land Administration System in Zimbabwe (by S. Mberi, S., F. Mazwi and W. Chambati)" *The Standard*, 15 November 2020.

in the administration of agricultural land that is vested in the state", as enshrined in the 2013 Constitution of Zimbabwe in Chapter 16(297)(1)(a).

Land administration overlaps and rivalries also strongly need to be dealt with to enhance an efficient land management structure with clear roles and responsibilities in dealing with disputes. This chapter observed the existence of several central and local government agencies involved in the whole process leading to administrative conflicts resulting in apathy, excessive bureaucracy and various allegations of abuse of power and resources. The key issues which have been identified include inconsistent policy, lack of accountability and transparency, unfair allocations, misidentification of land for acquisition, switching of target groups to the disadvantage of the most (land-)needy, and generally the slow pace of redistribution.

Land information management

Land information, which should be provided for in the formal land information management system (LIMS), is also currently not publicly available, which stimulates disputes and conflicts about land boundaries and ownership among farmers. The Zimbabwe Land and Agrarian Network (ZiLAN) through its land tenure cluster recommended publicising the land management information in a centralised database as a sure way of reducing the disputes.[4] Furthermore, to avert the emergence of new land conflicts and disputes, there is need to strengthen the capacity of LAS to enforce acquiescence with lease and permit conditions in the new resettlement areas.

Gender issues

A policy study by the Sam Moyo African Institute for Agrarian Studies (SMAIAS) also noted that there is a mal-representation of women in land administration boards, which is a hindrance to women's voices at policy level. A recommendation from ZiLAN was the need for a 50% representation of women in boards, as specified in the 2013 constitution. The representation of different categories of women in the land boards will enable other women to speak to their different needs from the grassroots level, including in chief's and district development coordinator's advisory boards (Mberi et al. 2020).

---

4   Ibid.

Community involvement

The study showed that a systematic and consistent bottom-up approach to participation by the rural communities has been virtually not present at all stages in various planning processes. The affected communities were not involved in the identification of alternative lands in cases of evictions, but it was rather imposed on them, for example in the case of Arda Transau. There is strong need to respect the rights of the communities through involving them in decision-making to seek a mutual consensus when evictions orders are passed.

8. Conclusion

The evictions, dispossessions and relocations of rural communities have been discussed and the fundamental causes exposed from peer evictions to state-induced displacements through its ties with capital, both local and international, in the name of 'development'. Despite the nature of evictions, whether for development purposes by the state or private capital, on farming land or residential land, an efficient land administration system that guarantees tenure security is critical. The existence of an effective land administration system that safeguards the rights and responsibilities of land rights holders is critical for any effective land tenure system, which guarantees landholders' security against any form of dispossession. A lesson from international experiences and acclaimed global best practice lies within the development and implementation of the Fit-for-Purpose (FFP) land administration system that embraces and is closely tied to the Global Land Tool Network's (GLTN) Social Tenure Domain Model (STDM) and range of land rights principles (see Moyo and Maguranyanga 2014). There is a strong need to adopt new approaches to land registration in order to enhance the implementation of a range of land rights at scale. The FFP land administration system, which also is anchored on spatial, legal and institutional frameworks with minimum rigidity and bureaucracy, is poignantly towards addressing the "what" and "how" questions of land tenure administration system using a flexible and incremental improvement approach (Enemark, McLaren and Lemmen 2016).

This chapter has illuminated that diverse land disputes have been universal across all land tenure categories with most disputes linked to lack of clear, durable and enforceable land rights (see also Chambati and Mazwi 2020). Furthermore, it was observed that the permit system which is given to the settlers is an administrative procedure without fundamental legal rights for the settlers. It gives the government organs and officers very wide discretion without giving the permit holders legally enforceable rights to land. The fact that most land occupants in the new resettlement areas have insufficient documentation to prove land ownership, with some holding onto temporary offer letters, suggests that their land rights remain uncertain and vulnerable to dispossessions by the state, businesses and influential individuals. As a result of poorly defined and provisional land rights, some settlers in communal areas, A1 and A2 have been exposed to continuous eviction threats and serious land ownership disputes. This calls for a lasting solution to address all forms of land disputes and the recent development by the Zimbabwe Land Commission to decentralise its offices and land dispute resolution functions is a critical move towards the development of an efficient and viable land dispute resolution framework.

Furthermore, it is critical to acknowledge, as emphasised by others like Hart (2002), that the traditional accumulation by dispossession that has shaped a myriad of countries in the global South, and Zimbabwe in particular, impoverishes the rural communities through evictions which further worsens their social inequality. Chambati et al. (2018) made similar observations that land dispossession led to increased landlessness among peasants in Sub-Saharan Africa, resulting in their inability to meet social reproduction needs, including food and other social requirements. Accumulation without dispossession buttressed by industrialisation and rural development can set a successful developmental path as evidence has shown in China and other East Asian countries. This points to the need for a major shift and rethink of practices by the Government of Zimbabwe towards development policies and strategies that enhance the wellbeing of the rural communities and the general population at large, beyond just the land tenure issues.

References

AIAS Baseline Survey (2007). "Inter-district Household and Whole Farm Survey Data-base", African Institute for Agrarian Studies.

Arrighi, G. (1970). "Labor Supplies in Historical Perspective: a Study of the Proletarianization of the African Peasantry in Rhodesia", *Journal for Development Studies*, 6(3), pp.197–234.

Bedi, H. P. and J. L. Cea (2019). "Women and Development-Forced Evictions: Realities, Responses and Solidarity", *Development in Practice*, 29(8), pp.1040-1052

Buka, F. (2002). *A Preliminary Audit Report of Land Reform Programme*. Harare: Government Printer.

Chambati, W., F. Mazwi and S. Mberi (2016). "Land, Agriculture and Extractives in Zimbabwe: an Overview", in Friedrich-Ebert-Stiftung (ed.), *Extractives and Sustainable Development II: Alternatives to the Exploitation of Extractives*. Harare: Friedrich-Ebert-Stiftung.

—— (2018). "Agrarian Accumulation and Peasant Resistance in Africa", in V. Gumede (ed.), *Inclusive Development in Africa: Transformations of Global Relations*. Pretoria: Council for the Development of Social Science Research in Africa.

Chambati, W. and F. Mazwi (2020). "Towards a National Gender Sensitive Land Policy in Zimbabwe: Issues for Consideration", Sam Moyo African Institute for Agrarian Studies (SMAIAS), Zimbabwe Land and Agrarian Network (ZiLAN).

Chingano C., T. Mereki and N. Mutyanda,(2015). "Chinese Investments, Marange diamonds and 'Militarised Capitalism' in Zimbabwe", Global Labor Column.

Chingarande, S. (2006). "Women and Access to Land in the Context of the Fast Track Land Reform Programme", African Institute for Agrarian Studies.

——. (2007) "Law and Gender Inequality: The Politics of Women's Rights in Zimbabwe". Department of Sociology, University of Zimbabwe.

Dhliwayo, O. and R. Joala (2020). "Land Tenure Insecurity in Zimbabwe Exposes Rural Communities to Intimidation and Arbitrary Evictions", Institute for Poverty, Land and Agrarian Studies.

Enemark, S., R. McLaren and C. Lemmen (2016). "Fit-for-Purpose Land Administration Guiding Principles for Country Implementation", United Nations Huma Settlements Programme.

Fisher, W. F. (1999). "Going Under: Indigenous Peoples and Struggles against Large Dams". *Cultural Survival Quarterly*, 23(3), pp.29–32.

Gaidzanwa, R. (2011). "Women and Land in Zimbabwe". Conference Paper, Why Women Matter in Agriculture, Sweden, 4-8 April 2011.

Government of Zimbabwe (2017). *Deeds Registry Act, Chapter 20:05*. Harare: Government Printer.

—— (2014). *Statutory Instrument 53 of 2014, Agricultural Land Settlement (Permit Terms and Conditions) Regulations*. Harare: Government Printer.

—— (2013). *Constitution of Zimbabwe Amendment (No. 20) Act*. Harare: Government Printer.

—— (2004). *Land Survey Act, Chapter 20:12*. Harare: Government Printer.

—— (2002). *Communal Land Act, Chapter 20:04*. Harare: Government Printer.

—— (2002a). *Land Acquisition Act, Chapter 20:10*. Harare: Government Printer.

—— (2002b). *Rural Land Act, Chapter 20:18*. Harare: Government Printer.

—— (2002c). *Rural District Councils Act, Chapter 29:13*. Harare: Government Printer.

—— (2002d). *Customary Land and Local Courts Act, Chapter 7:05*. Harare: Government Printer.

—— (2001). *Traditional Leaders Act, Chapter 29:17*. Harare: Government Printer.

—— (2001a). *Agricultural Land Settlement Act, Chapter 20:01*. Harare: Government Printer.

Hart, G. (2002). *Disabling Globalization: Places of Power in Post-apartheid South Africa*. Berkeley: University of California Press.

Harvey, D. (2003). *The New Imperialism*. Oxford: Oxford University Press.

Hwami, M. (2010). "Neoliberal Globalization, ZANU PF Authoritarian Nationalism and the Creation of Crises in Higher Education in Zimbabwe", *Journal of Alternative Perspectives in the Social Sciences*, 2(1), pp.59–91.

—— D. Madzanire and E. Hwami (2018). "Chiadzwa Resistance to Development Dispossession: Kleptocracy and Rural Struggles in Zimbabwe", *The Journal of Rural and Community Development*, 13(3), pp.1–19.

Kapoor, D. (2012). "Human rights as Paradox and Equivocation in Contexts of Adivasi (Original Dweller) Dispossession in India. *Journal of Asian and African Studies*, 47(4), pp.404–420.

Konyana, E. and M. Sipeyiye (2015). "Complex Moral Dilemmas of Large Scale Projects: The Case of Macdom-ARDA Chisumbanje Ethanol Plant Project in Chipinge, South–Eastern Zimbabwe", *International Journal of Sustainable Development*, 18(4), pp.349-360.

Mazwi, F., R. Muchetu and M. Chibwana (2017). "Land, Agrarian Reform in Zimbabwe from a Transformative Social Policy Perspective". *Africanus: Journal of Development Studies*, 47(1).

Mazwi, F., W. Chambati and K. Mutodi (2018). "Locating the Position of Peasants under the 'New Dispensation': a Focus on Land Tenure Issues", Sam Moyo African Institute for Agrarian Studies.

Mberi, S. and F. Mazwi (forthcoming). "Land Struggles in Zimbabwe", in W. Chambati, F. Mazwi and B. Monjane (eds). *Land Struggles and State Repression*. Mimeo.

Moyo, S. (2011). "Three Decades of Agrarian Reform in Zimbabwe", *Journal of Peasant Studies*, 38(3), pp.493−531.

—— (2011a). "Land Concentration and Accumulation after Redistributive Reform in Post-settler Zimbabwe". *Review of African Political Economy*, 38(128), pp.257−76.

—— (2009) "Emerging land tenure issues in Zimbabwe", African Institute for Agrarian Studies.

—— (1995). *The land question in Zimbabwe*. Harare: SAPES Books.

—— and B. Maguranyanga (2014). "Assessment of Zimbabwe's Land Administration System and Options for the Future", Land Studies Commissioned by the World Bank through the Agriculture Sector Technical Group (ASTG), funded by the Analytical Multi-Trust Donor Fund (A-MTDF).

—— and P. Yeros (2005). "The Resurgence of Rural Movements under Neoliberalism", in S. Moyo and P. Yeros (eds), *Reclaiming the Land: The Resurgence of Rural Movements in Africa, Asia and Latin America*. London: Zed Books.

—— and P. Yeros (2005a). "Introduction", in S. Moyo and P. Yeros (eds). *Reclaiming the Land: The Resurgence of Rural Movements in Africa, Asia and Latin America*. London: Zed Books.

—— W. Chambati, T. Murisa, D. Siziba, C. Dangwa, K. Mujeyi, and N. Nyoni (2009). "Fast Track Land Reform Baseline Survey in Zimbabwe:

Trends and Tendencies, 2005/6", African Institute for Agrarian Studies.

Neutens, J. J. and L. Rubinson (2002). *Research Techniques for the Health Sciences*. San Fransisco: B. Cummings.

Palmer, R. (1977). *Land and Racial Domination in Rhodesia*. Berkley: University of California Press.

Raftopoulos, B. (2006). "The Zimbabwean Crisis and the Challenges for the Left". *Journal of Southern African Studies*, 32(2), pp.203–219.

Rukuni, M. (1994). *Report of the Commission of Inquiry into Appropriate Agricultural Land Tenure Systems*. Harare: Government Printers.

—— and P.B. Matondi (2014). "Zimbabwe's Land Policy, Governance and Administration Options in Support of the Ministry of Lands and Rural Resettlement's Action Plan (2014-2016)", Land Studies commissioned by the World Bank through the Agriculture Sector Technical Group (ASTG), funded by the Analytical Multi-Trust Donor Fund (A-MTDF).

Scoones, I., N. Marongwe, B. Mavedzenge, F. Murimbarimba, J. Mahenehene, and C. Sukume (2010). *Zimbabwe's Land Reform: Myths and Realities*. Harare: Weaver Press.

Shivji, I. G., S. Moyo, W. Ncube, and D. Gunby, (1998). "National Land Policy Draft. A Draft Discussion Paper Prepared for the Government of Zimbabwe". Ministry of Lands and Agriculture, Food and Agriculture Organization of the United Nations.

SMAIAS Survey 2013/14 (forthcoming). "Land Use, Agricultural Production and Food Security Survey: Trends and Tendencies, 2013/14", Sam Moyo African Institute for Agrarian Studies.

Tucker, V. (1999). "The Myth of Development", in R. Munck and D. O'Hearn (eds), *Critical Development Theory: Contributions to a New Paradigm* (pp.1–26). London: Zed Books.

Utete, C. M. B. (2003). *Report of the Presidential Land Review Committee on the Implementation of the Fast Track Land Reform Programme, 2000-2002*. Harare: Government Printer.

Interviews

- Interview with PYD representative, May 2020. Telephone interview with the PYD director.
- Interview with a Chief, August, 2020. Telephone interview with Chief (Name withheld for anonymity).

- Interview with Councillor, August, 2020. Telephone interview with Councillor from Chipinge district.
- Interview with Villager, August, 2020. Telephone interview with a displaced villager from Chiadzwa.
- Interview with RDC officer, August, 2020. Telephone interview with Chipinge Rural District Council office.
- Interview with Villager, January 2020. Personal interview with Chisumbanje villager (name withheld for anonymity)

II

COLONIAL EXPERIENCES

4

One Dam, Two Different Relocation Processes: The Case of Kariba, 1956-1961

Terence M. Mashingaidze

1. Introduction

The Tonga's Kariba Dam induced displacements from the ecologically rich Zambezi riparian, where they practiced flood recession agriculture, were fraught with poor planning and discrepancies on the river's northern and southern banks (Scudder 1962, 1981, 1993; Colson 1971; Mashingaidze 2013, 2019). Besides displacing the Tonga at short notice, the Central African Federation government grossly underestimated the numbers of the displacees. In its 1951 annual report, the Central African Council on the Kariba/Kafue Hydroelectric Power Committee estimated that only 14,300 to 15,000 Africans in Northern Rhodesia and Southern Rhodesia[1] would be affected by inundation. The report further indicated that "no provision has been made in the estimates for the establishment of these persons, but it is understood that suitable land is available in local territories for this purpose" (Soils Incorporated Limited 2000, p.29). As it turned out in 1956, the actual number of people to be relocated was 57,000 (Scudder 1993, p.15) which translated to 23,000 and 34,000 displacees on the Zambezi River's southern and northern sides respectively.

At the time of displacement, the Federal Power Board (FPB), the institution mandated by the Central African Federation authorities to spearhead the Kariba Dam project, also disregarded the displacees'

---

[1] Northern Rhodesia is now Zambia and Southern Rhodesia is now Zimbabwe.

welfare. Whatever funds it provided for relocation could only be used for the Tonga's physical removal and direct compensation for losses incurred during dislocation, rather than to improve living conditions by providing schools, health facilities and agricultural extension services in the new places (Leslies 2005, p.119). The FPB, which viewed the displacees as an expensive nuisance (Scudder 1993, p.15), left the responsibility of relocating the Tonga under the control of the two countries' respective native affairs departments. This failure by the FPB to formulate uniform policies and binding standards for treating displacees partially explains, I argue, the paradoxical discrepancies in the relocation and post-relocation experiences of the Tonga in Northern and Southern Rhodesia. Northern Rhodesia's Westminster controlled colonial authorities consulted the Tonga, whereas the self-governing and colour bar driven white authorities in Southern Rhodesia simply expected the Tonga to go to the adjoining uplands to find habitable alternative land. The Southern Rhodesian government did not offer any compensation to the Tonga, while in Northern Rhodesia the compensation was inadequate. This chapter therefore disentangles and analyses these two territories' underexplored different treatments of the Tonga during their displacements.

By showing Northern Rhodesia's consideration of the Tonga's welfare, this chapter is not simplistically implying that their relocations were successful. In fact, successful resettlement is nearly impossible because it means "achieving not just a minimal restoration of the pre-displacement levels, but also significant improvement in displacees' livelihoods, above their pre-project levels" (Cernea 2008, p.3). The Northern Rhodesian government relocated many Tonga people to areas with poor soils and erratic rainfall, which exposed them to increasing food shortages and even famine (Siamwiza 2009, p.322). The majority of the Tonga that settled far off the lake encountered severe water shortages and difficult social and economic adjustments in their new arid environment. This new environment differed from the well-watered Zambezi riparian, which guaranteed secure food supply all year round for the Tonga. Nevertheless, the Northern Rhodesian government showed some partial sensitivity to the prospective Tonga displacees' welfare. A juxtaposition of these northern relocations against what transpired on the southern side of the Zambezi River will reveal how inconsiderate the Southern Rhodesian government was towards the Tonga under their jurisdiction.

This chapter is divided into four sections. In order to have a full grasp of the two territories' inconsistent Kariba Dam induced relocation processes, the first section explores their distinct administrative histories from the beginning of colonial rule in the 1890s. The second section, interrogates the Gwembe Native Authority's (GNA) negotiations and bargains with the Northern Rhodesian colonial administration for a favourable relocation outcome. The third section shifts the gaze to Southern Rhodesia, where the Native Affairs Department simply avoided any attempts at negotiation with the Tonga. The native affairs officials simply ordered the Tonga on their side of the Zambezi to relocate without compensation and adequate planning for decent livelihoods in the adjoining uplands. The last section shows the Zimbabwean Tonga's initial experiences in the dry uplands that were prone to tsetse flies and crop marauding wildlife.

2. Unpacking the Kariba Dam's different relocation processes: the historical antecedents

The paradoxically divergent Kariba Dam induced displacements in Northern and Southern Rhodesia can best be understood by appreciating their equally different colonial histories. From the imposition of British rule in the 1890s, which was spearheaded by Cecil John Rhodes' chartered British South Africa Company (BSAC), the two territories of Northern and Southern Rhodesia gradually evolved contrasting cultures of state power, 'native' policies and land ownership regimes. Ultimately, the Northern Rhodesian administration became somewhat accommodating to African interests, while their Southern Rhodesian counterparts developed apartheid like governance structures by shunning any pretensions of respecting African political and economic aspirations. These administrative traditions, which influenced the conduct of the 1950s relocations of the Tonga in their respective territories, were also caused by the BSAC's divergent economic designs and investments in the two territories.

In Southern Rhodesia, the BSAC sought to establish a settler colony with a permanent European population in the same way as in Kenya, South Africa and possibly the self-governing or dominion territories of Canada, New Zealand and Australia. Soon after the imposition of colonial rule, there was a rapid influx of Europeans who quickly parcelled out land to themselves. These indiscriminate land seizures compelled the British government to pass the Order-in-Council of 1898 that called the BSAC to provide adequate and suitable land for the indigenous population. The

Order-in-Council led to the creation of native reserves, whose boundaries were well defined by 1902 (Weinrich 1971, p.10). Much of the land reserved for Africans was infertile and dry. This European onslaught against African ownership and access to prime land intensified in the 1930s with the passage of the Land Apportionment Act (LAA) in 1931. The Act apportioned nearly 50% of the land to the tiny white population, whose numbers never went beyond 5% of the country's population throughout the colonial era (Rukuni 1994, p.16). Perhaps the most significant impact of LAA was that it triggered what Alexander, McGregor and Ranger (2000, pp.45-60) call "institutional violence" in the form of country-wide evictions of Africans on European designated land.

Contrary to the above situation in Southern Rhodesia, the BSAC had partial interest in Northern Rhodesia. Its initial interest was to develop it as a purely black colony in the mould of British colonies in West Africa. According to Ian Henderson, Northern Rhodesia's "original raison d'être was as a labour reserve for the developing white areas of Southern Rhodesia and South Africa" (Henderson 1974, p.295) at least up to the mid-1920s. Nonetheless, between 1904 and 1911 a total of 159 farms had been established between Kalomo in the south and Broken Hill, now Kabwe, in the north (Phiri 2006, p.11). Essentially, Northern Rhodesia never attracted a significant white population and much of the land remained in African hands. The British government also established legislative mechanisms to safeguard African land ownership. For example, in 1930 the Secretary of State for Dominion Affairs, Lord Passfield, issued a memorandum that was contentious to Europeans which indicated that in the case of conflict between African and European concerns, 'native' interests took precedence.

By the time of displacement in 1956, only a sixth of the land in Northern Rhodesia was either European owned or Crown property. The rest of the country was demarcated into 'Native Reserve Land' in which European ownership was outlawed, and 'Native Trust Land' where European activities were only allowed if they benefitted the indigenous population. As shown below, these land ownership structures meant that the Tonga in Northern Rhodesia could not lose much of the land upon the emergence of the Kariba Dam. Some of them moved only a few miles from the shoreline of the new reservoir. On the southern side, the Southern Rhodesian Native Affairs officials pushed the Tonga to the far off dry uplands and declared the new lake area and its immediate vicinity European or state land designated for wildlife conservation or recreational purposes.

Besides the above opposing land ownership and economic interests, the two countries developed different local governance or native policies. In spite of claims to the contrary, the Southern Rhodesian government largely ruled Africans through the direct rule system. Native commissioners (NCs) were the central players in this regime of governance (Palley 1966; Holleman 1969; Blake 1977; John 1985; Passmore 2002). Thus in the days of BSAC rule, African chiefs "were effectively replaced by European bureaucrats and ordered to serve them as constables" (Weinrich 1971, p.11.). NCs allocated land to Africans, issued them with cattle permits, and at the same time procured labour for European settlers. They decided who was allowed to settle in a particular locality and governed the interactions between Africans and businessmen. The High Commissioner's Proclamation of 1910 extended their powers by granting them civil and criminal jurisdiction over Africans (ibid., p.10).

The native commissioners' authority extended over the whole economic and political life of Africans. As the government's principal representatives at district level, the NCs were charged with a variety of responsibilities that included "the collection of African taxes, arbitration in civil disputes and protector of the allocation of land; to the registration of births and deaths, locust control and vaccination against small pox". In practice, the NC was "required to be at the same time administrator, manager, agriculturalist, civil engineer, judge, psychologist, architect, builder, doctor and vet" (Hermans 1960, p.22). This all permeating rule of Southern Rhodesian NCs is what Mahmood Mamdani defines as the "brazenly arrogant' nature of direct rule. Such rule was based on the assumption that:

> ...all native tradition was backward and needed to be eradicated. From this point of view, the cultural state had to be wiped clean as a prelude to a new historical trajectory, one that would hold the promise of modernity and progress. That development had necessarily to lead to the Westernization of colonial society (Mamdani 1999, 1996).

Southern Rhodesian settlers buttressed this intrusive policy of direct rule with racially selective policies in accessing and utilizing resources, such as land and wildlife. The settlers' socio-economic marginalisation of Africans intensified from 1923 with the end of the BSAC administration of the two territories. Southern Rhodesian settlers began to enjoy much freedom from Westminster, they became virtually self-governing. What reserved powers the British government possessed over their affairs were hardly exercised except in a cautionary and consultative capacity (Parker 1972, p.40; Weinrich 1971, p.9; Gann 1961, p.64).

Northern Rhodesian administrators, on the other hand, differed from their southern counterparts by devolving powers to indigenous leadership through recognizing chiefs starting from 1893 (Phiri, pp.9-27; Gann 1964, pp. 34-49; Slinn 1971). They encouraged the formation of chief's courts to allocate land and settle local disputes and of African councils to spearhead community development. With the end of BSAC rule in 1923, Northern Rhodesia became an official British Protectorate under the tutelage of The Colonial Office. It expanded its policy of indirect rule by administering African affairs through chiefs, traditional self-governing institutions. In pursuit of this decentralisation, chiefs in various localities would come together under local councils or native authorities to formulate intra-community development projects. In the Zambezi Valley, the chiefs operated under the auspices of the Gwembe Native Authority, which was constituted soon after the end of BSAC rule in 1923. Besides the chairman, the Authority was composed of all the seven Gwembe Tonga chiefs, seven nominated and elected councillors and five special councillors responsible for portfolios such as health, public works, water development, agriculture, and education. Chiefs and the chief councillor appointed the special councillors. The district commissioner was an *ex officio* member of the Authority (Colson 1971, p.15, pp.17-24).

Generally, the Zambian Tonga had a negative attitude towards the Gwembe Native Authority from the moment of its inception. They saw it as a pawn of the colonial administration, and this aversion for the Authority emanated from two perspectives. Firstly, it was because the powers assumed by the Authority were foreign to the Tonga way of life. The Tonga did not have traditions of centralised and hierarchical power structures. Secondly, in the few years preceding relocation colonial administrators had used the Native Authority as a foil to counter the influence of Harry Nkumbula's popular nationalist organisation, the Northern Rhodesian African National Congress (ANC) that had been formed in 1948. These administrators projected the Authority as a more legitimate representative of Tonga interests compared to what they perceived to be the ANC's pretentious and rabble rousing upstarts. However, in the context of the impending Kariba Dam induced displacements the Authority negotiated important concessions for the Tonga in Northern Rhodesia.

3. The Gwembe Native Authority and the displacement of the Tonga in Northern Rhodesia

Informed by recent thinking on 'Development-induced Displacements and Resettlements' (DIDR), Thayer Scudder, who has been working on the post-relocation experiences of the Zambian Tonga since the 1950s, has argued that resettlement on the northern side of the Zambezi River was not very bad. Although the Northern Rhodesian government lacked resettlement management experience and faced constraints of inadequate personnel, equipment, funds, and insufficient time for planning and implementing the Tonga's relocations, they had "the political will to do a good job" (Scudder 2009, p.37). In fact, they pioneered a number of 'best practices' for resettlement schemes, such as involving displacees in relocation planning. The Northern Rhodesian government tackled the displacements in a slightly different way, with less of South Rhodesia's autocracy and more of consultative committee work through the Gwembe Native Authority (Howarth 1960). The Authority bargained with the government for favourable relocation outcomes.

Soon after the breaking out of the news about the Kariba Dam's construction in 1955, the Authority held several meetings to plan for displacement and to negotiate for the promotion of their post-relocation interests. Hezekiah Habanyana, the Authority's Chief Councillor, was a key player in these consultations. As the first Tonga university graduate armed with a diploma from Bristol University in the United Kingdom, he was an articulate and astute negotiator for the rights of his people. He was not intimidated by the largely imperious colonial officials. Under his steady guidance, the Gwembe Native Authority drew up a list of concessions they expected the Governor to guarantee before displacement. Essentially, they wanted government assurances of compensation for the impending loss of property and their right to choose areas to relocate as well as some guaranteed benefits from the emerging lake. A fractional list of the Gwembe Native Authority's expectations and the Governor's responses were as follows:

> **Gwembe Native Authority (G.N.A)**: That in moving people their choices shall be seriously considered before they shall be ignored

and where possible their second choices shall be found.

Governor of Northern Rhodesia (Governor): I agree.

(G.N.A): That the Native Authority properties, including communications, amenities, shrines and also individual personal properties shall be compensated in full.

Governor: All people who suffer on account of being moved will be given either money or something else appropriate.

(G.N.A): That should there be any new people or businessmen who will establish themselves along the dam, the Gwembe Tonga Native Authority shall have the right to collect licenses, levies, taxes and rents from them.

Governor: Government will not trouble the people about their land more than is necessary, but it wants the land to be kept well so that it does not lose fertility, because it is from there that the food must come for all time.

(G.N.A): That sufficient supply of food shall be given to the people who shall have to leave their gardens to open new lands during the resettlement period.

Governor: I agree.

(G.N.A): That every effort shall be made to remove tsetse flies in the proposed new resettlement areas.

Governor: I agree.

(G.N.A): That should there be any chance of the water not reaching the suggested flood-line, the people who have been moved from the unflooded areas shall have the right to return to their original places.

Governor: I agree (Howarth 1961, p.50-52; Colson 1971, p.21-23).

The Governor's complaisant responses to the Authority's queries assuaged the Tonga's anxieties about the forced departures from their homelands. The government agreed to allow hundreds of Tonga families to move back to the edge of the reservoir to reoccupy unflooded land (Scudder 2009, p.38) and to provide piped water to the few Tonga families that settled near the new lake. Habanyana later acknowledged at a commission of enquiry about the relocations that the GNA agreed to relocate and make way for the dam because they were satisfied with the Northern Rhodesian government's assurances of compensation and other benefits to accrue from the lake. "Our minds were clear then", he conceded, and "we knew that the government was taking the move very seriously and that every aspect of the problem was being considered in the interest of our people"[2] (Habanyana quoted in Howarth 1961, p.52).

In spite of these concessions and promises, some of the Zambian Tonga found it difficult to accept leaving their homes and fields. They could not give up their ancestral lands without fighting. In September 1958 some men attempted armed resistance at Chipepo in Chief Chisamu's area. Upon hearing about the Chipepo people's reluctance to relocate, Governor Benson visited the area to encourage the resistors to move and after some futile negotiations he then warned the Chipepo men that "The Queen's words must be obeyed. If they are not obeyed, it will be necessary to enforce them" (Clements 1959, p.147). The following altercations on 10 September resulted in colonial policemen and soldiers shooting to death eight people and wounding 34 others.[3] Elizabeth Colson observed that from this point the Tonga were a "shocked and frightened people", fully aware of their fate if they defied government (Colson 1971, p.15). These massacres at Chipepo reveal that even the moderately inclined Northern Rhodesian authorities that seemed pliant to African demands and concerns at the time of displacement had limits to which they could tolerate African defiance. Despite this violent setback, the relocation process unfolded without further destabilisation and the Northern Rhodesian government honoured some of their promises to compensate and safeguard the Tonga's welfare after displacement.

4. Compensation for the Zambian Tonga and access to the new Kariba reservoir

In early 1960, the Northern Rhodesian government negotiated with the Federal Power Board for a settlement of £1,374,000. Much of this amount was paid out in five instalments to the Gwembe Special Fund for local infrastructural development, such as irrigation schemes, veterinary services, water supply, and especially the development of the fishery on Lake Kariba's northern shoreline. On 14 October 1960 the Federal Minister of Power, Sir Malcolm Barrow presented £200,000 to the Gwembe Native Authority, by now known as the Gwembe Rural Council, for direct

---

2 Habanyana quoted in "Giant in the Jungle (by D. Howarth)", *The Saturday Evening Post*, 2 April 1960.
3 Ibid.

compensation for resettlement losses and any "hardships encountered in moving" (Soils Incorporated Private Limited 2000, p.32). The colonial administrators agreed to a simple formula of compensation for property lost during relocation, particularly huts and riverine fields. They paid £134 to every person displaced and £10 for every house deserted because of relocation or lost due to inundation. This curious figure of £10 for a Tonga hut was established by counting the average number of poles each hut required and the man hours needed to cut and carry the poles and grass and to build such huts. Prevailing remuneration rates for manual labour were also factored into the calculation of the amount. Compensation for the loss of riverine gardens was worked out on the basis of the cost of clearing forest land (ibid., p. xi and p.32).

The Northern Rhodesian government also compensated the Tonga for crops which they could have grown in the time spent building new huts and breaking new land in the new settlements. These tasks were thought to likely take six months (Scudder and Colson 1972, p.46). These uniform payouts were unfair because they disregarded the specific worth of Tonga homes and fields by assuming that they all had equal value. Such subjective compensation mechanisms reveal that in as much as the Northern Rhodesian government willingly engaged the Tonga in planning the relocation process, they could not avoid the colonial habit of patronizing Africans and homogenizing their interests.

Soon after displacement, the Northern Rhodesian government limited commercial fishing on the northern side of the emerging lake to Gwembe residents[4] as a way of safeguarding their access to the Kariba fishery. It also allowed the Gwembe Rural District Council the right to license and receive fees from the commercial development of the lakeshore. Non-Tonga people could only participate in the marketing of the fish, which was open to any other interested blacks, whites and larger commercial firms. The Northern Rhodesian government established measures of promoting Tonga participation in the fishery, such as their 1958 sponsorship of some Tonga men for a fishing familiarisation tour in the Luapula Province, which had a thriving fishing economy (See Gordon 2006). Experienced Bemba and Lozi fishermen from this region were later appointed to share with the Tonga their fishing skills (Colson

---

4 This was the case up to 1964 when the new Zambian government resolved that the Lake Kariba and its associated fisheries were national resources that had to be exploited by all interested citizens.

and Scudder 1988, p.29). The Department of Fisheries followed up on this tour by initiating training programmes for aspiring fishermen. For example, in 1961, the government with the assistance of Freedom from Hunger, a British non-governmental organisation, established an ice plant and skill enhancement centre at Sinazongwe to provide training in improved fishing methods, boat building and maintenance. The government also set up a loan fund which the Tonga could use to purchase boats and nets (Colson 1971, p.146).

To some extent the Zambian Tonga got these benefits because the Gwembe Rural District Council continued exerting its influence in promoting and safeguarding Tonga interests after relocation. For example, in 1960 the Council succeeded in stopping plans for a joint Southern and Northern Rhodesian enterprise, the Kariba Lake Development Company, to coordinate economic activities, especially fishery businesses, on the lake. The company was supposed to have monopolies on the export of fish from the Valley, control the lake based transport system between the two territories and fish approximately two-thirds of the bush cleared areas. The other remaining portion was going to be reserved for the Tonga, who could also fish for subsistence in company waters (Bourdillon, Cheater and Murphree 1985, p.18). The Northern Rhodesian government was in favour of the plans, but they had to give up the idea since the Gwembe Rural Council refused to endorse the proposal, which it saw as a threat to its trading prospects and water rights (ibid.). The Council strongly resented any Southern Rhodesian government's involvement in the lake, partly because they had marginalised the Tonga on their side of the lake by racially segregating the southern shoreline's access and usage.

Unlike in Northern Rhodesia, big white-owned commercial companies were the major beneficiaries of Southern Rhodesia's fishing policies (ibid.). This was because the Tonga in Southern Rhodesia did not have comparable leverage to bargain with their respective colonial government, which disregarded their interests both at the moment of displacement and when they had settled in the dry adjoining uplands. These differences in approaches to displacement reflect the two territories' differing orientations towards African interests. So how did the actual relocation of the Zimbabwean Tonga unfold between 1956 and 1959?

5. Zimbabwean Tonga's ill-fated displacement and vain opposition to relocation

Whereas the Northern Rhodesian government partially engaged with the Tonga displacees in planning the relocation process, the Southern Rhodesian Native Affairs Department officials simply avoided any attempts at negotiation. They ordered the Tonga on their side of the Zambezi River to relocate without compensation and adequate planning for decent livelihoods in the adjoining uplands. Sir Patrick Fletcher, Southern Rhodesia's Minister of Native Affairs at the time of displacement, self-righteously recalled one of the altercations about the modalities of displacement he had with an official from Northern Rhodesia in the late 1950s soon after the Chipepo massacres:

> I had an argument with the Secretary from the Colonial Office at Chipwepwe's [sic]. He said I was being inhuman in moving people in 18 months and not paying compensation, and we had arguments on it. I eventually told him that I was going to get my people out peacefully, and wasn't going to be forced to come and shoot them out, and he took umbrage at that and jumped into his [car] and cleared off.[5]

The Zimbabwean Tonga could not negotiate any resettlement package because their government had little regard for 'native' welfare. It had a deeply ingrained culture of institutionalised violence against Africans as evident in its exclusionary land distribution policies that disproportionately favoured members of the European community. On their part, the Southern Rhodesian Tonga failed to bargain for any displacement packages because of a crippling absence of structures and avenues for negotiation, such as existed in the form of the Gwembe Native Authority among their counterparts in the north. These institutional weaknesses were made worse by low literacy rates, which undermined their collective abilities to articulate their demands and negotiate with the Federal Power Board and the government.

The Zimbabwean Tonga's displacements without compensation confirm James Scott (1988, p.88) observation that for high modernist projects, such as the Kariba Dam, and the resultant resettlements to be realised,

---

5 National Archives of Zimbabwe hereafter NAZ ORAL/FL1, Sir Patrick Fletcher interviewed by D Hartridge in June 1971. *Chipwepwe* in the quotation refers to *Chipepo*.

civil society has to be prostrate or simply lack the capacity to resist these plans. As a community, the Tonga could not oppose the dam construction or salvage some compensation for displacement. They were a marginal and illiterate community that could not effectively engage the high-handed colonial state. These low literacy rates and absence of a critical mass of leadership in the mode of men like Hezekiah Habanyana of the Gwembe Native Authority was due to decades of neglect by the colonial government. It did not develop schools on the Zimbabwean side of the Zambezi Valley.

In spite of the above limitations and the Tonga's avoidance of confrontation when Sir Patrick Fletcher and Native Commissioner Ivor Cockcroft initially told them of their impending displacements in August 1955, they could not simply accede to the reality of displacements when they began in July 1956. They resorted to diverse ways of expressing disenchantment with the Kariba Dam induced displacements. These actions entailed outright refusal to relocate, disrupting and stymieing the progress of the bush clearing teams, and joining en masse Harry Nkumbula's Northern Rhodesian based African National Congress (ANC) which was against the construction of the dam.

To a large extent, the Zimbabwean Tonga's opposition to relocation was motivated by the need to safeguard a world that gave them physical and spiritual sustenance. Besides the riverine area being generally a bountiful environment, where water, food and medicinal plants were generally available, it also harboured shrines such as sacred groves and trees. Displacement from the Zambezi would mean loss of important ritual sites and shrines, malende, along the river. The Tonga had two types of malende. The first types of malende were man-made hut-like structures called kaanda (plural, twaanda or little huts). The other type of malende that are more important for the purpose of this discussion consisted of natural objects that had become sacralised as dwelling places for rain giving spirits that intervened with Leza, the god who controls all things (Colson 1962, p156). Such places included large and hollow fig and baobab trees, hills and rock outposts, caves, springs, groves, and water pools on the edges of the Zambezi River.

Desires to hold on to these sacred spaces pushed the people of Manjolo, Siachilaba and Siansali to constantly stop the vehicles of D.G. Vorster's team, the main contractor of bush clearing, from uprooting their malende, shrines and sacred baobab trees. The desecration and loss of shrines was a dangerous affront to ancestors. The Tonga thought that if they allowed the malende shrines to be destroyed or inundated, their ancestors would punish them in the new upland areas by plaguing them with droughts, marauding elephants, and crop eating pests, such as locusts. This opposition to the destruction of malende shrines compelled government administrators to make regular trips to the Zambezi to negotiate with the Tonga. Richard John Powell, the Gokwe based Native Affairs officer, used to intervene in resolving such disputes:

> I used to get an urgent phone call saying via Kariba, 'can you come down,' and it would be 175 to 200 miles for me to travel. I did this a number of times and I spoke to the people near the baobab and they'd explain to me they could not allow it to be felled because all the family spirits dwelt in this baobab. And I would have to talk to them for some hours and point out that if they left it the family spirits would all be drowned and they would all be under water and they'd be no use to them. The normal procedure was they'd say, 'well, go away and leave it tonight and we'll discuss it and come back to see us in the morning.' And almost invariably when I got back in the morning they would tell me that they'd been able to move the spirits in the night…'You can tell Mr. Vorster to go on with his bulldozing.' So we had no serious problems. Sometimes it held up work for a few days because I had to get down to the area.[6]

The most determined refusal to relocation was coordinated by Makaza, a village head under Chief Sinakatenge, and his people who declined to relocate, arguing that they were being "bluffed by the white man" who wanted to "pinch our land".[7] Confronted with this obstinate refusal to relocate, Richard John Powell had to arrange for armed police to force Makaza's people out of their village. These police burnt down the resistors' huts and compelled them into lorries that took them away to the uplands, together with their crops and other belongings. About 20 to 30 of the most agitated resistors were handcuffed and forced into the lorries. Makaza and

---

6　NAZ ORAL 227, Richard John Powell, 1915-1984, Interview by E.G Gibbons, Salisbury, 3 July 1978, 21 August to 5 September 1978. Powell was appointed Provincial Commissioner in 1965, Deputy Secretary for Internal Affairs in 1969 and Secretary in 1972.

7　NAZ ORAL/227, Richard John Powell interviewed by E.G Gibbons, Salisbury, 3 July, 21 August and 5 September 1978. Powell was appointed provincial commissioner in 1965, Deputy Secretary for Internal Affairs in 1969 and Secretary for Internal Affairs in 1972.

some of his people returned to their village three weeks later, only to find that the water had begun to flood their homes. Chief Mola and his people also left the Zambezi River plains when the rising waters of the Kariba Dam began approaching their homes (ibid.).

Besides strong attachment to the fertile fields, some of the Zimbabwean Tonga's opposition to relocation was motivated by nationalist agitations. The ANC activists from Zambia exploited Tonga antipathy towards the dam to mobilise support. They encouraged people to buy ANC party membership cards on the grounds that they were some kind of talisman that would halt the construction of the dam.[8] The ANC preposterously claimed that the spirits, particularly those of the fabled serpentine river god, *Nyaminyami*, would not allow Europeans to either take away ANC card holders from the river-bank[9] or allow them to control the Zambezi River. It would not countenance the obstruction of its pathway and habitation by mere mortals. In this case the ANC activists were simply exploiting Tonga religious sensibilities because of the *Nyaminyami's* elevated position in Tonga cosmology.

According to popular Tonga lore, in times of hardships and food shortages due to crop failures *Nyaminyami* would swim along the river exposing its body without revealing its head and tail to the people, allowing them to cut off chunks of meat from its body. This explains the serpentine fish's name *Nyaminyami*, which is the Anglicised duplication of the onomatopoeic word, *banyama*, meat. *Nyaminyami* saved people from starvation. Whenever it started moving from its purported lair at Kariba Gorge, there were some tremors in the valley which still persist. Scientists now claim that tremors experienced after the construction of Kariba Dam are a result of seismic adjustments due to shifts in water levels in the dam. Besides tremors, people sensed and saw its movement and arrival at particular spots along the river. The water would either turn red or be unusually still.[10]

This belief in the existence of *Nyaminyami* partly explains why most of the Tonga bought the ANC's party membership cards. With the passage of time these people realised that the ANC's claims of having the

---

8 The cards had differential pricing according to age, gender and position in society. Children paid 1/9d, women 2/6d, men 3/6d, village headman 10/-, and chief 3 pounds.
9 NAZ ORAL/FL1 Sir Patrick Fletcher interviewed by D. Hartridge in June 1971.
10 Personal interview with Siazabana Jacala Mwiinde, Siabuwa Turnoff, Binga, Zimbabwe, 13 November 2008 and 17 July 2009; Personal interviews with Chief Bayela Sikalenge, Binga, 8 July 2009.

powers to prevent the construction of the dam were simply unrealistic. The Southern Rhodesian government seriously considered these ANC attempts at destabilizing the relocations. Native Commissioner Cockcroft thought the ANC activists almost derailed the relocation process and he had undisguised hostility towards the party:

> The problem of inducing people to cooperate in a mass evacuation to new inland areas was made more difficult by the preaching of self-styled African politicians, who for personal financial gain were quite prepared to use the gullible BaTonka as mere pawns for their own ends---not heeding the possibility of loss of life if the people were induced to defy the plan to move them to new homes ahead of the advancing waters. At one period some 3 000 people decided to refuse to cooperate in the hope that such action would prevent the construction of the Lake. However, many meetings and patient discussions in due course persuaded the people to move (Cockcroft 1967, p.26).

By the early 1960s, the ANC's influence among the Zimbabwean Tonga had waned to the extent that the Native Commissioner complacently observed that the Tonga in the uplands had settled into a contented rural population that had little interest in politics. He continued that there was "very little interest shown in the African National Congress", although "an isolated minority still under the influence of Makaza, occasionally attempt to make themselves heard, but is treated with suspicion by their neighbours".[11] A combination of the failures of the ANC instigated opposition to relocation, threats of violence by the colonial state against resistors and the imminent reality of rising waters of the Kariba Dam compelled the Zimbabwean Tonga to concede to the reality of an unfamiliar world in the uplands.

6. A slipshod affair: the Southern Rhodesian government's planning for displacement

The Southern Rhodesian government did not make serious attempts to improve the livelihoods of the Tonga in the uplands. They relocated them without surveys to assess soil fertility, possible human-wildlife conflicts and the availability of adequate water supplies in the new areas. Rupert Meredith Davies, the Assistant Director of Agriculture, even labelled the

---
11 NAZ S2827/2/2/7 Volume 1. Report for the NC Binga, for the year ended 31st December 1959.

relocation exercise a slipshod affair in which the Tonga were displaced to a country "that was inhospitable, waterless, arid, in which only baboons, antelope and rhinoceros could live".[12] Tonga elders recalled the moment of displacement as a time when the "colonial government revealed its moral bankruptcy"[13] by dumping them "in the wild to survive in arid tsetse and wildlife infested forests".[14]

Native Commissioner Cockcroft coordinated the government's piecemeal road building, water provisions and tsetse clearances in preparation for the Tonga's move into the uplands. It constructed small earthen dams and drilled boreholes in many parts of the district for providing water for livestock and other domestic needs for the relocatees. However, most of these boreholes yielded little water because the water table was generally low in many of the prospective areas for relocation. This problem was worse in the Manjolo Plateau, where most of the boreholes could not produce any water, a situation that compelled the tight-fisted colonial government to spend £29,000 for pumping water from the Kariba Dam through a 10 km pipeline.

The Southern Rhodesian government did not execute these preparations for displacement by itself. It conscripted Tonga men for the excruciating work of cutting trees and the construction of the network of access roads to the various parts of the uplands. Although the colonial authorities fed these labour gangs, they paid them nominal wages. Because of this low remuneration and long hours of arduous hard work, many elderly Tonga equated this road construction work to chibhalo, slavery. They also recall the period as magamuna which means the time of cutting down trees.[15]

Since much of the uplands were tsetse fly infested, what the Native Commissioner termed the "Wild Fly Country"[16] in 1961, some of the Tonga labour gangs participated in anti-tsetse campaigns aimed at making the area

---

12 NAZ ORAL/241 Oral interviews with Rupert Meredith Davis, 17 November 1983.
13 Personal interviews with Tala Sinasenkwa, Tyunga, Binga, 15 August 2008. These same sentiments were echoed in additional interviews with Peter Sizemba, Godfrey Siamatende, Tyunga, Binga, 15 August 2008, Mpolokwa Sinakoma and Solomon Muleya, Sinakoma, Binga, 15 May 2009.
14 Ibid.
15 Personal interviews with Finos Mudimba, Sinamagonde Binga, 19 June 2009 ; Siakuba Muzamba, Sinamatelele, Binga, 23 July 2009 and Million Munenge and Stephen Ncube, Sinamatelele, Binga, 23 July 2009; See also Philemon Munkuli quoted in Michael Tremmel, 1994. *The People of the Great River: The Tonga Hoped the Water Would Follow Them*, Gweru: Mambo Press, p.34.
16 NAZ 2827/2/8/1, District Annual Reports, 1961.

conducive for human habitation and livestock rearing. The colonial state employed three tsetse clearance measures. First, there was massive game destruction, particularly in Kariyangwe, east of Pashu and along the Busi River between 1957 and 1959. The aim was to create game free corridors between game parks, areas of tsetse concentration and areas where people were to reside. Ironically, these killings happened simultaneously to the much celebrated animal rescue mission 'Operation Noah'.

Clements (1959, p.184) suggests that for every animal that was rescued in Operation Noah, at least two, during the same period, were being killed in the uplands. According to David Howarth, government hunters slaughtered 2,239 animals in these anti-tsetse operations.[17] Second, the Veterinary Department, whose resident entomologist and experimental station were based at Kariyangwe, hired 'fly boys' to physically check and destroy tsetse flies and their eggs.[18] Many Tonga were involved in this 'hand-catching' of tsetse flies. The third anti-tsetse control measure was the use of organochlorophine insecticides, such as the environmentally harmful pesticide dichlorodiphenyltrichloroethane (DDT). This method entailed the spraying, using low fly small airplanes, of the insecticides in tsetse fly resting places. This aerial spraying method was mainly used in the Lubu-Kariyangwe valley, where the government spent close to £42,000.[19] Although these anti-tsetse campaigns made the uplands habitable, they were inadequate because by the time of the Tonga's relocation the tsetse had not been fully sprayed out. As a result, people displaced to the Siachilaba, Sikalenge and Simuchembu areas lost their cattle to tsetse induced trypanosomiasis.[20]

Besides the forced labour in the road and earthen dam constructions, the Tonga endured the burdens of travelling long journeys by foot to the uplands to identify suitable places. Men from the same village undertook numerous long distances on foot scouting for ideal places with good soils and reliable water supplies to set up their homes. They would carry mealie meal, relish and cooking pots for preparing meals along the way. Upon identifying good spots, some of these men built temporary shelters of

---

17 "Giant in the Jungle (by D. Howarth)", *The Saturday Evening Post*, 2 April 1960.
18 For extra details on this method see C Teesdale, 1940. "Fertilization in the Tsetse Fly, Glosina Palpalis, in a Population of Low Density," *Journal of Animal Ecology*, 9(1), p.24-26; see also NAZ S2827/2/2/6/3, NC Binga Annual Reports 1958.
19 Dick Hobson, *Kariba Notes*, p.55.
20 Personal interviews with Mariah Mutale, Siachilaba, Binga, 18 July 2009 and Josiah Shuma, Samende, Binga, 20 July 2009.

poles and thatch as markers for showing others that such places had been chosen. Since areas with good soils and abundant water supplies were difficult to find in the uplands' forbidding ecological milieu, many people, such as Fainos Munkuli of Siachilaba, ended up resigning themselves to establishing their new homes in whatever vacant spots they found:

> We saw that the area was not good, it was dry and the soils were infertile but we could not keep on moving scouting for better land. We had no choice and the pressure for us to leave the valley was getting more intense. State officials wanted us out of the Valley before the waters of the Kariba reservoir began rising.[21]

People who settled in the Siachilaba area hated the place because of its lack of water and they registered their disenchantment with Native Commissioner Cockcroft, who made futile promises to build small dams, drill boreholes and even provide them with the waters of the Kariba Dam through pipes. "People were very negative about this place but Cockcroft cajoled us", Chief Mujimba Siachilaba recalled. He continued that "... though we were sceptical Native Commissioner promised us better lives. He did all he could to make us move and when people complained about the scarcities of water he said water will follow you".[22] The government made promises to relocate them to the Busi River plains in the Sinamagonde or Lusulu area. The beginning of the country's liberation struggle in the 1970s scuttled these plans (Manyena 2003, p.22).

Upon identifying suitable places, the Tonga men and their chiefs would inform Native Commissioner Cockcroft of the selected places. The Native Commissioner then provided trucks for the transportation of property and small stock, such as mbelele, sheep, goats, and chicken. Some of these animals suffocated along the way. In most cases old men, women and children were driven in the trucks, while younger men and boys walked along with the livestock to the new places.[23]

7. The Zimbabwean Tonga's renditions of their departures from the Zambezi riparian

The Tonga were reluctant to leave for the uplands for a variety of reasons. Some did not want to leave their fertile fields in the ecologically rich

---

21 Personal Interview with Fainos Munkuli, Siachilaba, Binga, 12 July 2009.
22 Personal Interview with Chief Mujimba Siachilaba, 9 August 2009.
23 Personal interview with Luwo Mudenda, Siachilaba, Binga, 9 August 2010.

riverine zone, where water was readily available. Others could not envision the possibility of severing ties with their relatives on the northern side of the Zambezi River. Relationships and networks were much stronger across the river than along it. People had fields on the other side of the river and they regularly crossed the river in their dug-out canoes to visit friends and relatives and to partake in religious ceremonies, funerals, and beer and work parties. In this way the river was a communication highway rather than the barrier or the border that it came to symbolise after the construction of the Kariba Dam. Magoyela Mudimba recalled her people's sentiments at the point of departure from the Zambezi by saying:

> We travelled in the lorry burdened by our thoughts of the forced removal. We were removed by force and faced so many difficulties. We were leaving our best friends and relatives behind in Zambia and we would no longer be able to see them. How will we help them when they are troubled by the spirits? We left our big and beautiful villages, our homes, our fertile fields, our fish, our animals, our river. We left our precious life behind in the flooded waters. We did not want this to happen to us (Tremmel 1994, p.38).

Before leaving their homes by the Zambezi River, elderly men performed propitiation ceremonies to inform their ancestors about their departures. Sinamagulu Muchimba recalls that "when the time came for us to be removed, we organised ceremonies to inform our ancestral spirits that we had to settle elsewhere. When we reached our other part of the world, we also performed ceremonies and informed our spirits that we had now settled in the new area. We asked them to continue to look after us" (Tremmel, p.35). These supplications did not ease elderly men and women's anxieties because "when one is old, it is indeed a terrible thing to be separated from your long past; when you die, to be condemned not to join the welcoming throng of your ancestors, but to wander alone in a land which is empty of the dead" (Clements 1959, pp.92-93). Among the Tonga there exists a strong emotional bond between individuals and the territory of their ancestors. The desire to live there is equalled only by the desire to be buried there (Lan 1985, p.20).

Elderly Tonga women recalled the dislocations with much anger because they were hasty and often poorly planned. This meant that people settled in the wildlife infested uplands before they had built any houses for their families. Families slept in the open, exposed to weather elements and dangerous animals, such as lions, elephants, buffalo, hyenas, and leopards. Elena Mumpande recalled these anxious experiences by noting that "our family was not prepared when we reached the new area chosen by our chief. We were just dumped in the middle of a forest. Father had to cut some branches for our shelter for the first nights" (Tremmel, p.41). Women, such as Siazabana Jacala-Mwiinde, argued that the Southern Rhodesian administrators did not care much about the Tonga's welfare because

> ...the Native Commissioner and his assistants simply told us to go up there, to the *Lusaka* [Uplands], and locate suitable places with good soils and water. Such places did not exist, there were no good soils and sufficient water supplies were hard to come by. These people treated us like docile *mbelele*, sheep, which are driven from one place to the other without consultation. We struggled to make this *lusaka* place livable, we had to build homes and clear new fields all at the same time.[24]

As a way of alleviating the effects of the immediate hardships of displacement, the government granted a two year moratorium on taxation to the Tonga men. It also supplied the displaced people with maize, milk, beans, and salt for two years after relocation. This food was to compensate for deficiencies arising in the initial period. The government presumed that beyond these two years the Tonga would have established themselves and adjust to their new environments to be self-reliant. In addition to the food, the government provided free medical attention and drugs and regular free but inadequate inoculation of livestock against the tsetse fly induced disease, trypanosomiasis (Neshaw 1961, p.23). The Tonga were sceptical about this tax and food relief, which they assumed to be an attempt by the government to hoodwink them and atone for the pains it had caused them. For example, Solomon Mutale argued that "the colonial government gave us food so that we would not feel bad about moving from homes by the river because they wanted us to forget our former way of life. It was a way of blinding us" (Tremmel, p.41).

The Tonga's relocations to the uplands coincided with the designation of unfenced wildlife sanctuaries by the Kariba National Parks and Tourism Committee.[25] This committee met for the first time in January

---

24 Personal interview with Siazabana Jacala-Mwiinde, Samende, Binga, 17 July 2009; Majita Mudenda, Samende, Binga, 02 August 2009 and Siabulembo Libanga and Munsaka Chichelo, Tyuunga, Binga, 20 July 2009.

25 Chizarira National Park was designated as a non-hunting area in 1938, Chete Safari

1956 to examine the anticipated Lake Kariba's potential value as a tourist attraction and to consider the viability of establishing game sanctuaries (Soils Incorporated Private Limited, p.92). The Committee acknowledged recognition of the Tonga's needs for good land by noting that Sijarira (Chizarira) and Matusadonha Range, which would have lake frontage, had little agricultural potential, were of no value for resettlement and were virtually unpopulated. Such claims were not entirely true because these new wildlife sanctuaries not only had fertile soils and well-watered spots, but they had been traditional hunting grounds for the Tonga.[26]

N.C. Cockcroft attempted to help the Zimbabwean Tonga by opposing the establishment of these game parks in the uplands. He particularly opposed the idea of creating Chizarira Game Park in Binga where the majority of the relocatees were going to reside. He felt that concern over animal casualties stimulated by Operation Noah was misplaced. Rather, he emphasised human casualties to man-eating lions and depredation of crops by marauding elephants and argued that "the fact remains that dangerous game and humans cannot exist together" (McGregor 2010, p.119). The failure by Cockcroft's fellow colonial bureaucrats and planners to take heed of his advice consigned the Tonga to a fate of perennial food deficits induced by crop eating animals, such as elephants that easily strayed from their designated domains. In Northern Rhodesia, there were no plans for similar wildlife conservation zones in areas close to the lake.

By the end of 1961, the Native Commissioner complacently noted that the Tonga had peacefully resigned to their fate in the uplands, which made them reluctant to support emerging African nationalist movements:

> Binga is indeed fortunate in being 'an island' of peace amidst the stormy seas of politics. The youthful elements when away at work absorb a degree of industrial and political discontent but on return home this is soon lost in the atmosphere of tribal and family contentment. The family is too concerned with the problem of home life and food production to waste time or thought on matters concerning industry and Government. He has no overstocking problems, no land shortage that outpourings of the NDP or other

---

as game reserve in 1963, as well as Lake Kariba and the shore line that was put under the central Government Authority after the creation of Lake Kariba in 1957/8.

26 Once the Department of National Parks and Wildlife Management declared these areas game reserves and permitted hunting and photographic safaris in 1958, it became criminal for the Tonga to enter or exploit wildlife resources in such spaces without the required expensive special licenses.

movements fall on deaf ears. The recent decision to ban the NDP was welcomed by all, many Chiefs drawing attention to the fact that more severe sentences were essential to damp the ardour of the town '*tsotsi*' whose aim was to terrorize the more stable law-abiding native of his own.

However, the Tonga were not content with their deprived circumstances in the arid and wildlife infested upland homes.

8. Conclusion

Through a comparative analysis of the Northern and Southern Rhodesian governments' Kariba Dam induced displacements of the Tonga in their respective domains, this chapter has unpacked the scholarly silences on the different relocation programmes undertaken by the two administrations. The Northern Rhodesian government engaged the Tonga through their Gwembe Native Authority to plan for the displacees' compensations and in putting in place mechanisms that guaranteed Tonga benefits from the emerging Lake Kariba. However, this does not mean that displacement was not painful for these Zambian Tonga because by its nature displacement entails expropriation of land and asset dispossession, "it decapitalises the affected population, imposing opportunity costs in the forms of lost natural capital, lost human capital and lost social capital" (Cernea 2008, p.6). In Southern Rhodesia, colonial administrators simply pushed out the Tonga on their side of the lake without any restitution and post-relocation mechanisms for sustainable livelihoods, such as irrigation schemes. They did not compensate the Tonga for losses of fields, huts and livelihoods due to displacement. Although the Zimbabwean Tonga waged vain and disorganised attempts at resisting dislocation, they could not negotiate for compensation and guaranteed access to the fisheries of the Kariba Dam because they were largely an illiterate marginal community without the requisite bargaining skills to engage the imperious European administrators. This neglect of the Tonga by the colonial government continued after their settlement in the uplands.

References

Alexander, McGregor, J. and T. Ranger, T. (2000): *Violence and Memory: One Hundred Years in the 'Dark Forests' of Matabeleland*. Portsmouth: Heinemann.

Blake, R. (1977). A History of Rhodesia. London: Eyre Methuen.

Bourdillon, M. F. C., A. P. Cheater and M.W. Murphree (1985). *Studies of Fishing on Lake Kariba*. Gweru: Mambo Press.

Cernea, M. M. (2008). "Reforming the Foundations of Involuntary Resettlement: Introduction", in M. M. Cernea and H. M. Mathur (eds), "Can Compensation Prevent Impoverishment: Reforming Resettlement through Investments and Benefits Sharing". New Delhi: Oxford University Press.

Clements, F. (1959). *Kariba: The Struggle with the River God*. Gateshead-on-Tyne: Northumberland Press Limited.

Cockcroft, I. G. (1967). "Kariba,", *NADA: The Southern Rhodesian Native Affairs Annual*, 9(4).

Colson, E. and T. Scudder (1988). *For Prayer and Profit: The Ritual, Economic, and Social Importance of Beer in Gwembe District, Zambia, 1950-1982*. Redwood City: Stanford University Press.

Colson, E. (1971). *The Social Consequences of Resettlement: The Impact of the Kariba Resettlement upon the Gwembe Tonga*. Manchester: Manchester University Press.

——(1962). *The Plateau Tonga of Northern Rhodesia: Social and Religious Studies*. Manchester: Manchester University Press.

Gann, L J. (1964). *A History of Northern Rhodesia, Early Days to 1953*. London: Oxford University Press.

Gann. L.H. (1961). *The Birth of a Plural Society: The Development of Northern Rhodesia under the British South Africa Company 1894-1914*. Manchester: Manchester University Press.

Gordon, D. (2006). *Nachituti's Gift: Economy, Society and Environment in Central Africa*. Madison: University of Wisconsin Press.

Henderson, I. (1974). "The Limits of Colonial Power: Race and Labor Problems in Colonial Zambia, 1900-1953", *Journal of Imperial and Commonwealth History*, 2(3).

Hemans, H.N. 1960. *The Log of a Native Commissioner*. Bulawayo: Books of Rhodesia.

Holleman, J. F (1969). *Chief, Council and Commoner*. London: Oxford University Press.

Howarth, D. (1961). *The Shadow of the Dam*. London: St James Place.

John, M D. (1985). *The Governmental System in Southern Rhodesia*. Oxford: Oxford University Press.

Lan, D. (1985). *Guns and Rain: Guerillas and Mediums in Zimbabwe*. Harare: Zimbabwe Publishing House.

Leslie, J. (2005). *Deep Water: The Epic Struggle Over Dams, Displaced People and The Environment*. New York: Farrah, Straus and Giroux.

Mamdani, M. (1999). "Commentary: Mahmood Mamdani Responds to Jean Copan's Review," *Transformation*, 36.

—— (1996). *Citizen and Subject Contemporary Africa and the Legacy of Late Colonialism*. Princeton. New Jersey: Princeton University Press.

Manyena. S, B. (2003). "Missing the Tonga: The Impact of the Land Reform Programme in Binga District", Unpublished paper.

Mashingaidze, T M. (2019). "The Kariba Dam: Discursive Displacements and the Politics of Appropriating a Waterscape in Zimbabwe, 1950s-2017", *Limina: A Journal of Historical and Cultural Studies*, 25(1).

—— (2013). "Beyond the Kariba Dam Induced Displacements: The Zimbabwean Tonga's Struggles for Restitution, 1990s-2000s", *The International Journal on Group and Minority Rights*, 20.

McGregor, J. (2010). *Crossing the Zambezi: The Politics of Landscape on a Central African Frontier*. London: Heinneman.

Neshaw, W.T. (1961). "Kariba Resettlement (Southern Rhodesia)", *NADA: The Southern Rhodesian Native Affairs Annual*, 37.

Palley, C. (1966). *The Constitutional History and Law of Southern of Southern Rhodesia 1888-1965*. Oxford: Clarendon University Press.

Parker, J. (1972). *Rhodesia: Little White Island*, London: Pitman Publishing.

Passmore, G C. (2002). *Hidden Conflict: A Documentary Record of Administrative Policy in Colonial Zimbabwe, 1950-1980*. Westport: Praeger.

Phiri, B J. (2006). *A Political History of Zambia: From the Colonial Period to the Third Republic, 1890-2001*. Trenton: Africa World Press.

Rukuni. M. (1994). "The Evolution of Agricultural Policy", in M. Rukuni and C. Eicher (eds), *Zimbabwe's Agricultural Policy*. Harare: University of Zimbabwe Press.

Scott, J. C. (1998). *Seeing Like a State: How Certain Schemes to Improve the Human Condition Have Failed*. New Haven: Yale University Press.

Scudder T. (2009). "Resettlement theory and the Kariba Case: An Anthropology of Resettlement", in A. Oliver-Smith (ed.), *Development and Dispossession: The Crisis of Forced Displacement and Resettlement*. Santa Fe: School for Advanced Research Press.

—— (1993). "Development Induced Relocation and Refugee Studies: 37 Years of Change and Continuity among Zambia's Gwembe Tonga", *Journal of Refugee Studies*, 6(2).

—— (1993). *A History of Development in the Twentieth Century: The Zambian Portion of the Middle Zambezi Valley and the Lake Kariba Basin*. Binghamton: Institute for Development Anthropology.

—— (1981). "What it Means to be Dammed: The Anthropology of Large-Scale Development Projects in the Tropics and Sub-Tropics", *Engineering and Science*, 54(4).

—— and Colson, E (1972). "The Kariba Dam Project: Resettlement and Local Initiative", in H. R. Bernard and P. J. Petto (eds), *Technology and Social Change*. New York: Macmillan Company.

—— (1962). *The Ecology of the Gwembe Valley*. Manchester:Manchester University Press.

Siamwiza, B S. (2009). "When Community Resources are Expropriated: Loss of Common in the Gwembe Valley, 1958-2004", in R. Modi (ed.), *Beyond Relocation: The Imperative of Sustainable Resettlement*. New Delhi: Sage Publications.

Slinn, P. (1961). "The Role of the British South Africa Company in Northern Rhodesia, 1890-1924", *African Affairs*, 70.

Soils Incorporated Private Limited. (2000). "Kariba Dam: Zambia and Zimbabwe", Report Prepared for the World Commission on Dams.

Teesdale, C (1940). "Fertilization in the Tsetse Fly, Glosina Palpalis, in a Population of Low Density", Journal of Animal Ecology, 9(1).

Tremmel, M. (1994). The People of the Great River: The Tonga Hoped the Water Would Follow Them. Gweru: Mambo.

Weinrich, A. K. H. (1971). Chiefs and Councils in Rhodesia. London: Heinemann.

5

Colonial and Post-Colonial Relocation Experiences of Two Headmen in Zaka District

Francis Muromo

1. Introduction

Whereas in recent years drought and civil wars in Africa have received widespread coverage as fundamental causes of population movement, colonial dispossession of land and development projects are slowly being forgotten as other causes of current challenges being faced by some local communities. This case study explores the experiences of two headmen due to colonisation and development-induced displacements (DIDs), namely Headmen Muromo and Headman Gupure under Chief Bota of Zaka District in Masvingo Province. The colonial DIDs, characterised by the construction of Bangala Dam on Mutirikwi River and the establishment of commercial cattle and game ranches for white farmers in Chiredzi District, had serious consequences for the two headmen and their communities that last until today.

The case study attempts to answer the following questions: firstly, how did the forced displacement of one Headman Gupure affect his livelihood portfolios and those of the host communities in Chief Bota's area of Zaka Rural District? Which socio-economic activities were affected by an influx of displaced persons in the host community and what were the effects of these changed norms? How did competition over livelihood opportunities relate to social cohesion and conflict between the displaced and the hosts?

How have the conflicts been resolved?

In an attempt to answer these research questions, primary and secondary sources of data were used. Primary sources included interviews with key informants, such as the two current headmen, the Zaka District Administrator and the Masvingo Provincial Administrator. Secondary sources included a review of literature on displacements that took place globally and locally.

2. Contextual background

The construction of Bangala Dam at the Mutirikwi River for sugarcane plantation irrigation in the south-eastern lowveld resulted in the movement of local communities who resided along this river. The dam lies in Masvingo District, south of Masvingo Town. It was built between 1961 and 1963 to provide irrigation water to the farming estates of Triangle and Hippo Valley, where the main crop has been sugarcane.

Illustration 1: The location of Bangala Dam along Mutirikwi River

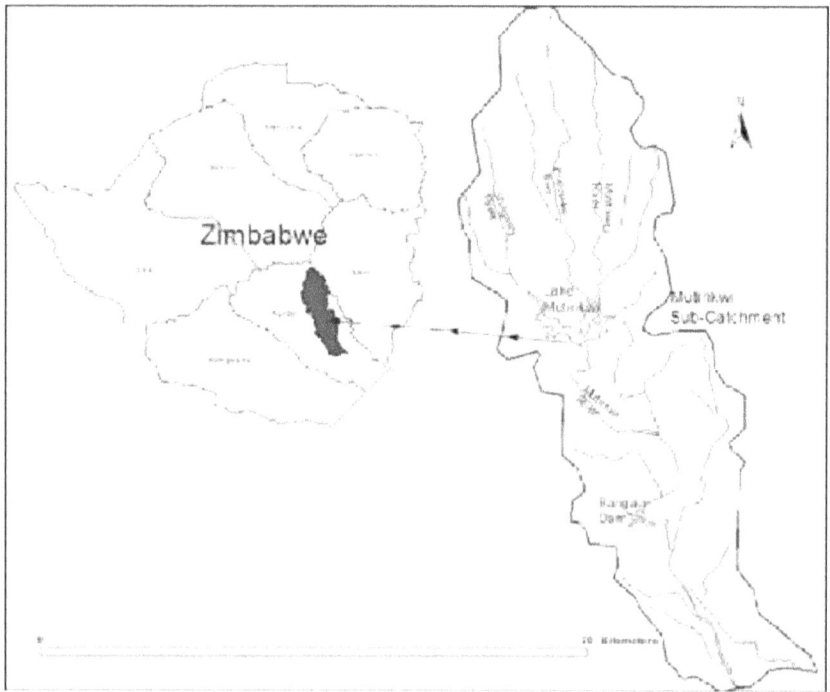

The movement of people to pave way for this development project had a ripple effect on adjacent communities in Zaka District, which also shared

Mutirikwi River as a boundary with Masvingo District. During this time Headman Gupure and his subjects moved from the Sviba Area in then Zaka Native Area (now Zaka Rural District) to the Romwe Area in Chiredzi District in search of farming as well as grazing land for their livestock. However, their stay in Romwe was short-lived, as they were forcibly relocated back to Zaka Native Area to pave way for commercial cattle and game ranching projects for some white settlers in the new area.

In the Zaka Native Area, Headman Gupure initially settled in Headman Marangarire's area where subsistence farming in small grains and livestock were the main source of livelihoods. His arrival in the area resulted in competition over grazing land which culminated in tensions and conflict with the host community. Sometimes these tensions ended up in nasty verbal and physical exchanges between the arrivals and the host community. Because of the fights, the local white Native Commissioner then moved Headman Gupure and his subjects again to a more sparsely populated area about 10 km away. The new area was under the jurisdiction of Headman Muromo. The relocation of Headman Gupure to this new area did not solve the problem. It was simply transferring a problem from one headman to another.

3. Justification

This case study was motivated by the following reasons: firstly, as a son of Headman Muromo, the writer witnessed several exchanges between his father and Headman Gupure over farming and grazing land as he grew up. The exchanges were so intense that at one point in 2010, there was a physical exchange between the two headmen's subjects over a piece of land to which they all claimed ownership. This attracted police intervention as Headman Muromo had an autochthonous claim to the area, while Headman Gupure indicated that he was resettled by the colonial administration. The former claimed that his grandfather's grave was about three hundred metres from where Headman Gupure's homestead was, while the latter indicated that no one resided in the area at the time he was resettled. Interestingly, the former cited natural boundaries, such as mountains and rivers, as his boundaries, while the latter cited colonial infrastructure in the area, such as a road and a dip tank, as his boundaries.

To avert further clashes between the two headmen, they were both afforded an opportunity to present their cases before a council of chiefs of Zaka District. Although the council recognised that Headman Gupure was a headman in his right, they ruled that he had no jurisdiction over the area in dispute. They advised him that if he wanted to repossess the Romwe Area, he had to take advantage of the land reform exercise that was currently taking place to reclaim what was his. It is interesting to note that despite that historic ruling by the chiefs, it is more than five years now and Headman Gupure has not moved an inch from where he was initially settled by the colonial administration. However, some of his subjects have long moved to other areas with a few having relocated to Romwe in the aftermath of the Fast Track Land Reform Programme (FTLRP).

Secondly, a newspaper article in the *Masvingo Mirror* in June 2018 on verbal exchanges between Chief Tsovani of the Shangaan people and Chief Bota of the Shona over ownership of the Romwe Area in Chiredzi District further ignited the researcher's interest to embark on the study. The article, entitled 'Chief Tshovani to fight the expansion of Bota Chieftainship', highlighted a verbal exchange over an area where Headman Gupure claims to have come from. The two chiefs were attempting to expand their jurisdiction in the aftermath of Zimbabwe's historic land reform programme ushered after independence in 1980.

Headman Gupure, who is currently under Chief Bota in Zaka District, had always pointed out that he was forcibly relocated to where he is now to pave way for cattle and game ranching for white farmers in the yet to be created Chiredzi District. The relocation occurred during the formal colonisation of Zimbabwe by European settler occupation. This process lasted 90 years, from September 1890 to Zimbabwe's independence in April 1980.

The headman's claim to the Romwe area met a lot of resistance from Chief Tsovani's subjects. The chief, in a bid to expand his boundaries, had resettled his people who also had an autochthonous claim to the area hence sucking in the two chiefs from the two districts.

The above reasons ignited the researcher's interest to establish the reality on the ground. It is hoped that the findings of this study will inform government officials as well as the local traditional leadership in their future endeavours.

4. Findings

4.1. How did the forced displacement affect the livelihood opportunities of the displaced and host communities?

The two headmen concurred that the main sources of their livelihoods were farming, rearing livestock, as well as hunting, since wild animals were plentiful then. They both indicated they grew small grain crops in the area, like rapoko, mhunga and sorghum. For Headman Gupure, the Romwe Area was arid and therefore ideal for cattle farming hence the huge herds of cattle he owned. This meant that when he was relocated to Headman Marangarire's area, the demand for land increased culminating into tensions and conflicts with the hosts. To ease pressure on land, the colonial government ordered them to destock. Both headmen indicated that their predecessors hotly clashed with the colonial administration as they felt that destocking was a colonial strategy of disempowering black people. The strategy was meant to force black people to go seek employment in newly created white people's cattle ranches.

After the relocation population increase on the land, more land had to be given to ploughing. This meant a reduction in the number of cattle each household held as grazing land became scarcer. Hunting also became less prominent as population increases moved wild animals in the area further away.

Asked about the legitimacy of their claims to the area, the two headmen were quite passionate, as highlighted by the following narration by Headman Muromo:

> I was born here. I inherited ownership of this area from my father. My forefathers were born and buried here. My boundaries include Zuzwi Mountain Range in the east and Rupiri River in the west.

Headman Gupure, on the other hand, pointed out that there was no one residing there when he was resettled in the area:

> From Romwe Area I was initially settled under Headman Marangarire but fights over farming and grazing land made the District Commissioner (DC) then to move me here. There were no people in the area and DC felt the place was ideal for us and our large heads of cattle. By then Headman Muromo was staying near Rudhanda Business Centre about three kilometres from my homestead.

The records at the District Administrator's office acknowledge that there are two headmen in the area under dispute, but there are no maps to show the boundaries between the two. The records also indicate that Headman Gupure moved into the area in the 1960s. This therefore confirms

Headman Muromo's claim that he resided in the area before Headman Gupure, further consolidated by the fact that the latter mentions colonial infrastructure like the road and dip tank as his boundaries, as opposed to natural features like mountains and rivers. What should be noted is that in the 1960s the area was sparsely populated hence Headman Gupure's claim that there was no one there at the time he was resettled.

The displaced people and the host communities were not directly involved in the resettlement process. They were not even consulted about the choice of the resettlement area. It was evident that the colonial government was in partnership with the white farmers hence resettling the displaced people on communal land not too far from white-owned farms so that they could easily access cheap labour.

Displaced families looked forward to a wide range of entitlements in terms of compensation from either the government or white farmers. Common forms of compensation ranged from transport cost, compensation for lost economic and non-economic assets, lost income and common property resources. In the end, the affected families received only two types of benefits, i.e. transport to move their assets and livestock from Romwe to Zaka Native Area and food once every four months until the next harvest. The food provided by the government to each family consisted of basic food items like maize meal, salt, beans, dried fish, and cooking oil. However, each relocated family had to construct its own shelter using pole and dagga material.

4.2. Which socio-economic activities were affected by an influx of displaced persons in the host community and what were the effects of these changed norms?

For the host communities, the coming of the displaced resulted in a strain on the available infrastructure like schools, clinics and dip tanks. There was also a strain on common property resources like grazing land. During the relocations, some children of the displaced families underwent a period of adjustment to new learning and teaching environments, with some children even dropping out from school. Enrolment in different schools also entailed additional costs to parents related to the purchase of new uniforms and ancillary costs.

The government did not build new schools or health centres in the settlement areas. People walked very long distances to schools and for health services. In fact, there were only two secondary schools for the whole of Zaka District during that time, namely St Anthony's Mission by the Roman Catholic Church and Jichidza Mission by the Dutch Reformed Church (now: The Reformed African Church).

Headman Gupure and his people also lost several economic and non-economic assets, for which they thought they could get additional compensation to what they got from the government. These included deep wells they had sunk at their homesteads, well-tended gardens, as well as mature fruit trees and woodlots to meet wood fuel needs in the future. They also had built granaries and cattle kraals. All these assets were not included in the official asset inventory and the headman was concerned that these assets may not have been evaluated appropriately.

Sonnenberg and Münster (2001) recommend the use of resource economists to do the valuation of non-economic assets. Headman Gupure and his people regret having left behind their ancestors' graves. They consider it an act of betrayal and felt that it was like casting away one's identity. The government did not pay out money to allow for exhumations. Reburial dates and sites as well as compensation for these were not decided. Such socio-cultural issues are the hidden costs of involuntary displacement which were not captured in the asset inventories.

Headman Gupure and his subjects indicated that the government told them that it would not cover costs for people opting out of the designated resettlement area. People opting out of the planned resettlement process would forfeit all forms of compensation. As a result, some of the displaced families went to other areas different from where their headman relocated. At the resettlement site, each family was allocated a sizeable area of dry land farming, which had not been cleared.

The relocation also disrupted social support systems, as in most cases the families were a collection of people who were not necessarily related. As a consequence, Headman Gupure and some of his subjects were separated from their relatives and neighbours, which undermined their social support structures by diffusing their social networks. Headman Gupure and his people were small-scale farmers dependent on agriculture for a living and for them livelihood options were limited in the new area of settlement.

4.3. How did competition over livelihood opportunities relate to social cohesion and conflict over land?

Since the year of the relocation, the two headmen have not enjoyed peace as tensions and conflicts over land increased in the area when both headmen's families grew in size. Apart from verbal exchanges over grazing land, there were also physical exchanges. Headman Muromo indicated that at one point he ploughed down Headman Gupure's maize crop on a disputed piece of land. This culminated in criminal charges being laid against him. These fights were mainly about the demand for land, but also spread to the administration of some traditional aspects in the area, such the observance of cultural rites and respect of ancestral shrines.

4.4. How have these tensions and conflicts been resolved?

Several hearings to resolve the conflicts between the two headmen were held by Chief Bota, but to no avail. The matter was referred to the Zaka District Administrator who referred the matter to the chiefs' council in his district as well as the Masvingo Provincial Administrator. After listening carefully to both sides, the chiefs' council resolved that although Headman Gupure was a headman in his right, he had no jurisdiction over the area he claimed ownership of. They recommended that all his subjects be transferred to Headman Muromo's jurisdiction, which the Zaka District Administrator implemented. The chiefs advised Headman Gupure that if he wanted to reclaim his ancestral land in Romwe, he had to take advantage of the current land reform programme that is under way.

Since Headman Gupure was an old man at that point, establishing a new home was next to impossible for him hence his continued stay in the area until he passed on. He was a heartbroken man after being stripped of his power. Some of his subjects deserted him and some have since relocated back to the Romwe Area, only to be confronted with a new problem. The area is now inhabited with the Shangani people, who also have an autochthonous claim to the area. This is what ignited a 'war of words' between Chief Bota and Chief Tsovani as alluded to earlier on.

5. Conclusions

- Apart from development projects, colonial land appropriation also contributed to the displacement of rural communities in Zimbabwe, as has been highlighted by the experiences of the two headmen. Of late, this has been exacerbated by globalisation and economic liberalisation driving the pace of development in African rural communities, who continue to bear a disproportionate burden of the cost of development projects. Development-induced displacements destabilise the affected communities and expose them to impoverishment risks.

- Displacement is a negative externality of development (WCD 2000). In the case of the two headmen, a lot of time and effort has been placed on trying to legitimise their claim to the land in question at the expense of developing the area. Both headmen concur that they are in a worse off situation than they were before. Because of overgrazing, they were forced to destock and because of the population increase the size of farming land per household was reduced.

- Governments and project developers often consider that their responsibility ends with payment of compensation. In Headman Gupure's case, he and his subjects were only provided with transport to the settlement area as well as some food packs once every four months until the next season. Once-off payment of compensation alone is never adequate to allow for sustainable rehabilitation of communities uprooted from their ancestral land.

- In Headman Gupure's case, the authorities should have incorporated an action plan that allowed the headman and his people to have sustainable livelihoods at levels above pre-displacement income. As noted in this study, before the displacement the headman and his people derived their livelihoods from crop and livestock farming as well as hunting. After relocation these were no longer viable livelihood options due to shortage of land.

- As noted in the study, during the relocations the families had great difficulty accessing basic services and amenities. The community was also fractured as social capital was dispersed. Consequently, relocated families were not clustered in the same way as at origin, which caused social dissonance. For Headman Gupure and his people, seeking recourse to their grievances is particularly difficult as new developments have taken place in the areas they came from.

- Income from agriculture is uncertain in a new environment hence there is a crisis of expectation tinged with frustration. Headman Gupure did not know how much money the affected people would be paid as compensation. The headman and his people were heavily dependent on the largesse of the authorities undertaking the relocation. If this is allowed to be the norm, this is likely to inculcate a dependency syndrome, which exacerbates the displaced families' socio-economic vulnerabilities, forestalling rehabilitation and adjustment.

6. Recommendations

From the above conclusions the study recommends the following:

- Dialoguing between the responsible authorities and the affected communities prior to relocations. The colonial government did not involve the affected communities and headmen in the relocation process which resulted in a myriad of conflicts between the host communities and the relocatees during the colonial period and beyond.

- Ensuring that livelihood initiatives be instituted before displacement to allow for displaced families to rebuild their livelihoods and reclaim their dignity. The authorities did not consider the livelihood options of the host communities and the relocatees. Both communities heavily depended on crop and livestock farming but instead of strengthening these, the colonial government curtailed them. Farming and grazing land got scarcer as the population increased. Furthermore, the government forced the communities to destock as a strategy to disempower them and make them seek employment on newly created white-owned cattle and game ranches.

- Adequate support infrastructure like clinics, schools and boreholes for the displaced should be placed in advance. Such an infrastructure will avoid the straining of existing facilities in host communities. In this particular case these issues were never attended to.

References

Sonnenberg, D. and Münster, F. (2001). "Research Topic 3: Mining and Society - Involuntary Resettlement", African Institute of Corporate Citizenship and Mining Minerals Sustainable Development Southern Africa.

World Commission on Dams (2000). Dams and Development. London: Earthscan Publications.

Interviews

- Interview with Headman Muromo at his homestead on 15 October, 2019.
- Interview with Headman Gupure at his homestead on 16 October, 2019
- Interview with Chief Bota at his homestead on 20 October, 2019
- Telephone interview with Zaka District Administrator on 5 November, 2019
- Telephone interview with Masvingo Provincial Administrator on 5 November, 2019

III

POST-COLONIAL EXPERIENCES

6

The Resettlement and Compensation of Displaced Households: A Case Study of Marovanyati and Causeway Dam Projects[1]

Chrispen Maseva

1. Introduction

Between October 2018 and February 2020, the Infrastructure Development Bank of Zimbabwe (IDBZ) has been monitoring the resettlement and compensation processes for two Government of Zimbabwe funded dam projects, namely Marovanyati and Causeway dams. Causeway Dam spans over two districts, namely Marondera and Makoni, while Marovanyati is in Buhera District. The two projects are part of the portfolio of the Public Sector Investment Programme (PSIP) in the water and sanitation sector, whose fund disbursement is managed by the IDBZ.

As is common with implementation of projects of this nature, the two projects caused displacement of communities that had, for many years, settled in the respective dams' basins. The projects inevitably disrupted these people's agro-based livelihoods and left some amongst them wondering if at all the projects should be termed developmental projects in view of the socio-economic scars they left on the affected people. This chapter outlines how the relocation and compensation processes

---

[1] Any views or opinions presented in this chapter are personal and belong solely to the author and do not represent those of people, institutions, companies or organisations that the author may be associated with in personal or professional capacity.

were undertaken and makes recommendations on how the processes can be improved in order to make future projects more sustainable.

2. Background to the relocation process

Marovanyati and Causeway dams are owned by the Government of Zimbabwe through the Zimbabwe National Water Authority (ZINWA). ZINWA has a mandate to ensure sustainable development and equitable distribution of the country's water resources to all Zimbabweans at an affordable price (Government of Zimbabwe 2010). Construction of dams in the country is therefore a function that falls directly under ZINWA's mandate areas.

Construction works on Marovanyati Dam started in 2003, but stalled due to lack of funding, and only resumed in 2013 under a contract with China Jiangxi Corporation for International Economic and Technical Cooperation. The construction of Causeway Dam started in 2016 also under a contract with another Chinese company, China Nanchang Engineering P/L. Marovanyati is meant to be the main water supply source for Murambinda Growth Point in the drought prone Buhera District. The dam will also supply water to planned and existing smallholder irrigation plots downstream of the dam. Causeway will provide irrigation water to the surrounding A1 model resettlement areas as well as some commercial farms in the areas around the dam. In the face of evident climate change, the two dams will go a long way in helping communities to adapt to the effects of climate change.

3. Institutional arrangements

The resettlement and compensation of people affected by government-financed projects involves several players. Prior to dam constructions, ZINWA as the responsible authority conducts a survey of the dam's basin to determine, among other things, the number of existing households and social infrastructure in the basin. Results of the survey are communicated to the Director of Valuations in the Ministry of Local Government, Public Works and National Housing and to the Director of Budgets in the Ministry of Finance and Economic Development. This communication is meant to trigger the valuation exercise from which the total budget required to relocate the affected people is derived.

Incidentally, ZINWA's parent ministry is the Ministry of Lands, Agriculture, Water and Rural Resettlement. It follows that as soon as

ZINWA compiles information about the number of people requiring relocation from the basin, both the Department of Lands and that of Rural Resettlement are simultaneously alerted of the need for alternative land on which to resettle the affected households. Administratively, the resettlement and compensation processes are handled by the District Development Coordinator (DDC), formerly the District Administrator. The DDC's office, like the Department of Valuations, falls under the Ministry of Local Government, Public Works and National Housing. There are therefore three government ministries and at least four different departments that are directly involved in the relocation and compensation, as shown in table 1.

Table 1: Institutional roles in the compensation and resettlement of 'Project-affected Persons' (PAPs)

Ministry	Relevant department/ entity	Responsibility
Ministry of Lands, Agriculture, Water and Rural Resettlement	ZINWA Lands	Carrying out surveys to determine households and social infrastructure to be relocated from dam's basin District Lands Officer is a member of the District Lands Committee, tasked with finding alternative land for resettling affected people
Ministry of Local Government, Public Works and National Housing	Valuations District Development Coordinator's office	Conducting valuation of all affected households and compiling the total budget required for relocation Administrative role: The DDC chairs the District Lands Committee which determines where to resettle affected people Receives and disburses compensation funds to the affected households
Ministry of Finance and Economic Development	Budgets	Avails funds to compensate the affected households

4. The relocation and compensation processes

4.1. *Relocations from Marovanyati Dam basin*

A total of 14 families were in the Marovanyati dam basin when construction works began in 2003. Even though construction works were suspended until 2013, the situation regarding settlements in the basin had still not changed when construction finally resumed ten years later. All the 14 families remained in the basin, oblivious of their fate. Available records show that asset valuation was only undertaken in October 2018. Families only became clear about the impending relocation during the valuation exercise. However, they still could not be relocated as alternative land had not been secured. Three options were considered with regards to relocation:

    a) Relocation within neighbouring villages

    b) Relocation to other areas within Buhera district

    c) Allocation of residential stands at Murambinda Growth Point

Plans to relocate the families were scuppered as the 14 homesteads were flooded in March 2019 following heavy rains that lashed the area at the back of Cyclone Idai. The families had to be rescued under emergency conditions, losing virtually everything that they had, including their food reserves. The sad development was covered by the national broadcaster, the Zimbabwe Broadcasting Corporation (ZBC), as illustrated below.

Illustration 1: ZBC coverage of the flooding

ZBC News Online @ZBCNewsonline · 26m

JUST IN: Marovanyathi Dam in Buhera is now spilling due to the heavy rains and houses in the vicinity have been destroyed. Rescue teams have been called in for assistance. The families are said to have ignored calls to relocate from the area during the construction of the dam.

4.2. Disbursement of compensation funds for Marovanyati Dam

All the 14 households received compensation from the government in October 2019, 7 months after they were rendered homeless by flooding.

Unlike other cases, where victims receive compensation equivalent to the estimated value of what they lost, in this case compensation was based on what the Ministry of Local Government, Public Works and National Housing called a 'rural model homestead', as shown in table 2.

Table 2: Proposed rural model homestead for affected households

Proposed structure	Value (USD)
1 x 3 bedroomed house with dining room (Asbestos roof)	11,500
1 x grass thatched round hut	2,000
1 x 2 squat hole blair toilet	1,200
1 x granary	3,446
Total	18,196

A valuation exercise done on the 14 homesteads by the Ministry had given each homestead an average value of USD $5,000. Victims of Marovanyati dam therefore got compensation that was more than three times higher than the assessed values of their homes. Much as this was a desirable development, the money was paid in local currency and had depreciated significantly when it was finally paid.

4.3. Relocations from Causeway Dam basin

Causeway dam displaced a total of 95 homesteads on the Marondera District side and a further 20 on the Makoni District side. Most of these families were settled in the area by the government in the early 1990s on individual plots averaging 6 hectares per household. Faced with the challenge of finding alternative land to resettle these families, the Ministry of Lands, Agriculture, Water and Rural Resettlement through the respective District Lands Committee responded by consolidating all the plots that were outside the dam's basin and then demarcating new, smaller plots averaging 2 hectares per household. The rationale for the reduction was that these plots will be put under irrigation hence farmers would not need 6 hectares. The re-demarcation of plots created enough land to resettle all the affected families.

4.4. Disbursement of compensation funds for Causeway Dam

Asset valuation for the affected households was completed in August 2018. Value of homesteads ranged from as little as USD $63 to as much as USD $239,792. The money was however only paid in November 2019 and in Zimbabwean Dollars at the rate of 1 to 1, although the Zimbabwean Dollar had lost considerable value against the USD. The valuation covered every immovable asset, including fruit trees. In addition, each family received a disturbance allowance amounting to 20% of the assessed value of the homestead. Most of the families felt that the compensation fell far short of what they needed to rebuild their lives. This was made worse by the fact that, despite the valuation being done in United States Dollar terms, payment was in Zimbabwean Dollars.

4.5. Challenges associated with the resettlement and compensation processes

The experiences of families displaced by Marovanyati and Causeway dams point to the following challenges that need to be addressed:

- Failure to include costs of relocations and compensation in the total project budget. Compensation and relocation costs should be integrated into the project budget. In both Marovanyati and Causeway dam cases, funds to compensate the affected families were only availed several years after commencement of construction works.
- Best practices require that compensation and relocation happen well before commencement of construction works. However, in the case of Marovanyati, funds to compensate the affected families only became available at the end of the construction period, 16 years from the date construction works began.
- Poor coordination between and within government ministries/ departments. Some of the people displaced by Causeway Dam were settled in the area in the early 1990s only to be displaced again in 2019. This could have been avoided if relevant government departments had a coordinated approach to development in the area.
- It is increasingly becoming difficult to find alternative land to resettle people displaced by development projects. This calls for more judicious use of land.
- There must be a way of ensuring that 'Project-affected Persons' (PAPs) benefit from projects that affect them negatively. The rationale is that the PAPs are not supposed to be worse off in terms of their socio-economic status, than they were before the project. In the case of Marovanyati, the displaced families are unlikely to derive direct benefits from the dam after having been settled upstream of the dam, more than 30km from the proposed site for a new irrigation scheme.

References

Government of Zimbabwe (2010). *Project Summaries under the Government's Investment Proposals for the Water Sector in Zimbabwe.* Harare: Government Printer.

Interviews

- Causeway Dam site - Mr Madondo (Resident Engineer)
- Office of the District Administrator Marondera District (Marondera) - Mr Masawi (District Administrator)
- Office of the District Administrator Makoni District (Rusape) – Mr Museka (Assistant District Administrator) and Mr Tarondwa (District Administration Officer)
- Manicaland Provincial Administrator's Office, Mutare – Mr Misi (Deputy Director, Local Governance) and Mrs Sithole
- Office of the District Administrator Buhera District – Mr Mushayavanhu (Assistant District Administrator)

7

Displacement Due to Urban Expansion in Mazowe District: Illustrations from Selected Urban Settlements

Joel Chaeruka

1. Introduction

Zimbabwe has been urbanizing at a rate of 1.6% per annum according to Mbiba (2017) and 2.0% according to the Population Projection Thematic Report (Zimbabwe National Statistics Agency 2015). This has led to significant urban sprawl (Dube and Chirisa 2012) and peri-urban settlements[1] which rapidly expand into surrounding rural areas. This chapter explores how urban centres in Zimbabwe are acquiring land to expand, the nature and types of urban expansions and how such expansions are causing development-induced displacements. The challenges created by this development and the impact on surrounding rural areas and the people inhabiting those areas are analysed based on the example of Mazowe District in Mashonaland Central Province.

According to Giorgi and Klos (2014) displacements can be caused by natural disasters, such as floods, drought and storms, but also by development initiatives, especially major infrastructure developments. Development-induced displacements come in many ways, e.g. dam construction, road construction, establishment of a new town, expansion of existing urban settlements, new irrigation schemes, promotion of

---

[1] Peri-urban settlements usually consist of low to medium density suburban areas with stands between 300m^2 and 2000m^2.

tourist facilities, or provision of social infrastructure. Of interest here is displacement caused by urban expansion or urbanisation and associated development. Urbanisation is based on acquiring and subdividing rural land for urban development.

The immediate needs of displaced people are shelter, food, health and education facilities. Furthermore, development-induced displacements trigger the issue of the right to property and fair compensation for loss of land and property, which can be complicated if there is poor security of land tenure. The displacement of people also raises the question of the effects on cultural sites and heritage. Cultural heritage is a legacy of physical objects or artefacts and intangible qualities of a group of society that they inherited from past generations, sustained in the present and preserved for the benefit of future generations (Ashworth et al 2007). In terms of spatial planning, tangible heritage is mainly of concern and should be accommodated in land use layout plans. Tangible heritage includes materials preserved in some physical form that one can touch or see, for example buildings, historic places, monuments, and cultural landscapes (Vecco 2010).

2. Research problem and purpose

2.1. Statement of the problem

Urbanisation in Africa has been the subject of several comprehensive case studies, e.g. Jonga and Munzwa (2010) in Zimbabwe, Bidandi (2018) in Uganda and Ukoje (2016) in Nigeria. However, rarely have such processes been linked to the issue of development-induced displacements and compensation of the affected rural people, who lose land due to changing land uses and settlement patterns in the context of peri-urban development and the transition from rural to urban land. This chapter tries to close this gap and also intends to explore the effects of urban expansion on tangible heritage. Thereby, the chapter tries to contribute towards understanding urbanisation in Zimbabwe in its totality.

2.2. Purpose and methodology

This chapter unpacks the Zimbabwean legal framework on urban development in rural areas and the relevant provisions regarding compensation of displaced people. Furthermore, the chapter presents the results of a study carried out in Mazowe District on the nature of urbanisation, forms of displacement, how these displacements are being mitigated, and which challenges arise in terms of compensation for displacement. The chapter focuses particularly on the manner in which the expansion of selected urban settlements was handled by the authorities in light of the need for compensation for the displaced, including the underexplored issue of compensation for tangible cultural heritage.

Data collection was done through desk research, studying layout plans, master plans, district development plans, and various reports. Interviews with informants and observations are the other methods that were used.

2.3. Specific objectives

a) To outline and analyse laws and policies regulating urban expansion, displacement and compensation from a planning perspective.

b) To establish the nature of urban expansions and resultant boundary changes that are taking place in the selected service centres in Mazowe District.

c) To analyse displacement issues resulting from urban development in Mazowe District and the forms of compensation offered to the affected rural communities.

d) To understand challenges evolving around the compensation for and protection of tangible heritage in Mazowe District.

e) To make recommendations on how to improve displacement and compensation processes related to urban expansion.

3. Legal framework for urban development and compensation in Zimbabwe

3.1. Relevant institutions and actors

Land is a key asset and the management, development, administration, and allocation of land involves a myriad of institutions and actors at national and local levels, including the Office of the President and Cabinet, the Ministry of Local Government and its various departments, the Ministry of Lands and Agriculture, the Ministry of Housing and Amenities, the Minister of State for Provincial Affairs, the Provincial Council and Provincial Administration, as well as local authorities, traditional leaders, the courts, the land commission, and parliament. In terms of the private sector, interested groups include land developers, various forms of cooperatives, banks, real estate companies, planning consultants, community based organisations, amongst others. Last but not least there are the individual citizens and communities with an interest in land, who want to be heard and listened to. As a result, a myriad of laws has been put in place to accommodate all those institutions and organisations and their different interests.

3.2. Laws and policies regulating the acquisition of rural land for urban development

The Constitution of Zimbabwe lists a number of rights in section 72 and brings up pertinent issues on land and agriculture in chapter 16 in light of property rights and the owners' rights as articulated in section 71. Accordingly, one can be deprived of property rights for reasons such as public interest, order, morality, defence or safety. Section 86 further clarifies conditions under which ownership rights and freedoms are overlooked in purchasing, expropriating and using land.

Primary law on handling acquisition in the context of urban expansion is covered by the Land Acquisition Act, mainly under section 3 which talks about acquiring land for various purposes, including urban/town development. In addition to this, the Regional, Town and Country Planning Act in sections 45-49 details how land can be acquired for planned urban development and the circumstances in which it can take place. Also the president has superseding rights of mining, infrastructure development, interruption of set existing public works and roads on a property and the right of repossession where compensation will be rewarded.

Sections 150-152 of the Urban Councils Act are informative on how an urban council can acquire and alienate land. Although section 205 of the Urban Council Act gives councils powers to carry out estate development, in terms of section 150(3) councils cannot acquire land not covered by a master or local plan unless granted express permission by the Minister of Local Government. Approved development plans in line with the Regional, Town and Country Planning Act, such as master plans, local plans and layout plans, can bring about change in development patterns. Development which transforms land from being rural to urban are addressed in sections 14, 17 and 40 of the Regional, Town and Country Planning Act.

However, additional conditions apply in terms of establishing urban land within communal land. In terms of section 10 of the Communal Lands Act the Minister of Local Government can set aside land for urban development through secondary legislation, such as a statutory instrument. This is supported by section 73 of the Rural District Councils Act which states that properly established townships should be enforced. Part III of the Communal Land Act states that council and traditional leaders are expected to agree on the allocation of communal land to users as well as any excision of communal land for urban development.

Accordingly, setting aside communal land for urban development requires secondary legislation by the minister as well as consultation of the Rural District Council (RDC). The assumption is that chiefs and headmen as ex-officio members of the RDC and ward committees, respectively, will make their inputs on behalf of the communities they lead. These conditions and options try to enable urban development, while also protecting other forms of land use. An example for the establishment of urban land within communal land is Statutory Instrument 379 of 1982, which gazetted a list of controlled development centres (growth points) across the country, such as rural service centres, business centres and district service centres.

At policy level, it is recognised that there is a need for urban development and that peri-urban areas will in future be part of the urban centres. As a result, mechanisms for acquiring and banking land for future urban growth were put in place. Subsequent housing policies supported incremental development as a development strategy to cater for peri-urban development, which may have put pressure on the demand for urban land.

3.3. Laws and policies on compensation for rural land acquired for urban development

The Constitution of Zimbabwe (2013) in its founding principles speaks of equitable sharing of land and protects land occupancy and property rights under sections 71 and 72. However, land can be compulsorily acquired for public purposes, such as urban development. If privately owned agricultural land next to an urban settlement is designated to be acquired and transferred to the local authorities through the Ministry of Local Government, the recipient local authorities are expected to pay full compensation to the owner. In the context of the Fast Track Land Reform Programme (FTLRP), the Land Acquisition Act distinguishes land acquisition for certain public interests, such as infrastructure and urban development, from land acquisition for resettlement on agricultural land. In the case of the latter, compensation is designated only for improvements on the land and not for intrinsic value of the land.

Part IV of the Regional, Town and Country Planning Act in Part IV addresses compensation issues, especially in acquiring land for urban development, and covers the procedure to be followed, while stating that fair compensation should be paid. Section 20 of the Land Acquisition Act states that reasonable compensation shall be paid, but does not define what constitutes "reasonable compensation". Reasonable compensation in line with the Land Acquisition Act also appears in section 220 of the Urban Councils Act according to which the authorities "shall pay compensation for loss of rights over land where one resides". Section 18 of the Rural District Councils Act points to the need to enforce compensation for acquired property and section 124 also provides rural councils with the option of borrowing to pay for compensation.

Although the need for compensation for the acquisition of private land in the public interest is clearly spelled out, with the restriction to compensation only for improvements in the case of land acquired for agricultural resettlement in the context of the land reform, the issue is more complicated due to the complex land tenure systems in Zimbabwe. Since occupants on state land, such as inhabitants of communal lands or resettlement areas, do not own the land they are permitted to occupy and use, they are not enjoying the same rights to compensation as private land owners.

If communal land is set aside for urban development, for example in the case of Statutory Instrument 379 of 1982, it is implied that the local inhabitants do not qualify to receive financial compensation for the land, which is vested in the President of Zimbabwe and has no intrinsic value since it cannot be purchased. However, section 12 of the Communal Land Act provides that compensation shall be provided in terms of alternative land or an agreement on compensation shall be reached. In terms of resettlement areas on commercial farms acquired through the Ministry of Lands as part of the land reform programme, the resettled farmers also do not qualify for compensation for the land.

4. Urban expansion and displacements in Mazowe District

4.1. Background

Mashonaland Central Province is one of the 10 administrative provinces of Zimbabwe. Mazowe District is one of the 63 districts in Zimbabwe and one of the eight districts in Mashonaland Central, the others being Bindura,

Shamva, Rushinga, Muzarabani, Mount Darwin, Guruve, and the recently created Mbire. Mashonaland Central Province has a population of 1.350.532 people (Zimbabwe National Statistical Agency 2012). According to the 2012 census, 198.966 people are living in Mazowe District and the inter census report projects an estimated 233.000 people (Zimbabwe National Statistical Agency 2015).

Mazowe District, which shares a border with Harare City, is the most populous district in Mashonaland Central Province. The province is mostly rural with only Bindura Town and Mvurwi Town (located in Mazowe District) qualifying to be part of the 32 self-administering towns of Zimbabwe in terms of the Urban Councils Act. The province being mostly rural is a catalyst to urban settlement development or expansion. Major service centres like Mount Darwin, Shamva, Guruve, and Kanyemba have the potential to expand rapidly or are already rapidly expanding.

Within Mazowe District, major service centres are Glendale urban, Nzvimbo District Service Centre, Concession urban and Mazowe urban. Minor centres that deserve attention in Mazowe District are Gweshe, Kanhukamwe and Christonbank. Nzvimbo, Kanhukamwe and Gweshe are within or abutting communal lands whilst the others are next to commercial farms, tourist sites or mining areas. Natural population increase and immigration into Mazowe District is putting pressure on urban settlement expansion and rapid peri-urban development is taking place.

Economic activities include maize, cotton, tobacco and soya bean farming, and the famous Mazowe orange orchards riding on an average rainfall of 864mm a year. Irrigation schemes have been set up to allow all year round market gardening and citrus fruit farming. Market gardening is wide spread to serve Harare City. Gold mining has attracted and is attracting large numbers of people into the district as artisanal miners. Rural urbanisation is gradually taking place to accommodate those attracted to the district as well as the natural population growth.

The majestic Mazowe River runs through the southern part of the district creating a picturesque valley as it meanders through the Great Dyke Lobe forming the north-eastern part of the high veld of Zimbabwe. Mazowe Valley and Enterprise Valley in Goromonzi have for a long time been protected for farming because of their good soils. The Mazowe Dam lends itself to tourist attraction in a district experiencing a mean annual temperature of about 21°C, which has caught the interest of developers.

In terms of spatial planning the Harare Combination Master Plan (HCMP) covers Mazowe Township and Christonbank only. These are covered as a mining town and a business centre (BC) respectively. The HCMP was prepared in 1992 and is no longer covering current development needs. The other centres do not have plans for the future. Decision-making is done by 34 councillors responsible for the 34 wards in the district with Chief Chiweshe, Chief Makope and Chief Negomo as ex officio members of the council.

Urban centres focused on in this study are Mazowe, Concession, Kanhukamwe and Nzvimbo. Nzvimbo is ranked as a District Service Centre (DSC), Kanhukamwe is a Rural Service Centre, Mazowe and Concession are mainly mining centres, although Concession has been turned into the administrative capital of the district thus side-lining Nzvimbo DSC.

4.2. Development plans in Mazowe District

One of the objectives of this study speaks to the nature of urban expansion that is taking place in selected service centres in Mazowe District. Are there development plans that are guiding development in these centres? As pointed out earlier, Christonbank and Mazowe are covered by the 1992 HCMP and Mvurwi is covered by a master plan. The rest of the service centres are covered by layout plans or some form of concept plans. This means that there is very little in terms of plans on how the various service centres should develop going into the future. As a result, developments happen ad hoc. This incremental mode of urban expansion and development puts land holders and land owners in a quandary whether to continue subsistence or commercial farming and hope their farming activities will be protected, or to jump on the subdivision band wagon and make hay whilst the sun is still shining.

The Mazowe Rural District Council (RDC) has been preparing district development plans. However, these have little detail and list projects that the district wishes to implement without being rigorously prioritised. District development plans are not being given attention as expected, partly because of apathy – plans are prepared but are not followed or implemented mostly because of financial problems and lack of resources to support the plans. Anyone can come up with a development idea creating a free-for-all situation which complicates the handling of development and subsequently compensation. The planning officer narrated, "we are using layouts, but our settlements are rapidly expanding, especially Concession and Glendale.

We need to prepare local plans to effectively guide development". The Planning Officer confirmed that they are making efforts to make sure that these statutory documents are in place.

Development plans and layout plans supported by the housing waiting list for Mazowe District indicate a demand for about 10,000 residential stands across the district. This means a sizable amount of land is to be put under new urban developments. A residential estate is accompanied by land demands for industrial, commercial, institutional, and recreational purposes. The new developments can only happen on land which is currently still under other forms of land use in the rural or communal areas. Rural population displacement is taking place and will continue to take place as urban areas develop.

4.3. Existing developments and development plans for Mazowe urban

Mazowe urban is an old settlement which has been in existence since the 1900s as a business centre serving Alice Mine and Jumbo Mine. Mazowe urban continues to be a service centre for the mining and farming communities. It is home to the oldest hotel in the country, the Mazowe Hotel (Ministry of Tourism). Mazowe Valley is also home to the Mazowe citrus fruit farming business. In 2014, the population was 9,966 people and the urban centre had over 2,000 stands.

There has been growing interest in the area. Mazowe urban is rapidly expanding with CBZ Bank servicing land to develop a residential estate. Other developers are coming in as well. Real estate companies like Robert Root are marketing stands in the area. Mazowe urban area is likely to expand by 950 residential stands. Mazowe Dam, which shares a boundary with the urban area and the picturesque mountain ridge and valley, has attracted a lot of interest from developers from Asia, America and Europe. Developers are interested in lodges, hotels and water based activities. Developers are interested in the area surrounding Mazowe Dam partly because the dam water is not as polluted as Lake Chivero west of Harare. Currently, the dam offers a number of recreational activities for both local and international visitors, who throng the area all year round. The RDC is interested in seeing the area converted into a prime tourist destination and the proposed tourist infrastructure/superstructure will be accompanied by a residential estate. The plans of proposed developments anchored by Mazowe Dam are ambitious though at a preliminary planning stage. The proposed developments are likely to be on privately owned land, land under ZINWA and land under the Ministry of Lands, such as acquired farms.

Mazowe is also a culturally rich location. The urban centre is flanked by a virgin forest of a variety of indigenous trees on the southern and western side, citrus farms on the eastern side and vast farmland to the north. Mazowe is strategically located in an area suitable for sight-seeing. Nearby is a game park with famous wildlife like rhino, giraffe, buffalo, and a variety of other species. The Inspiration Park is nestled in the mystic Shavarunzwe Hills and is being used as a venue for events, while the Botanic Reserve includes a variety of natural vegetation. The area is also known as the home of the spirit medium Mbuya Nehanda.

4.4. Existing developments and development plans for Concession

Concession is the administrative centre of the district with a population of 5,000 people. It is located next to a mine in an area where most of the land is used by commercial farms, partly on state land and partly on private land. The old section of the settlement is mostly residential with some offices and shops. Two residential schemes are going up on the western side of Concession. The declaration of Concession as the Mazowe RDC headquarters has encouraged urban expansion. It used to be mainly a service centre with some shops and workshops, but has started to rapidly expand with mushrooming residential, industrial and institutional stands. There are plans to create 1,400 residential stands in the Amandas, Highwood, Portlock and Rockwood areas. Some private subdivisions are taking place as well as infills. One of the big subdivisions for residential development has been put on hold by the Ministry of Land working together with the Ministry of Local Government, which could however be temporary.

In comparison with Mazowe, there are not many notable sites in terms of tangible cultural heritage in Concession. Concerns are on graves, forest patches, wetlands, and historical buildings. The settlement was based on a railway station linked to delivering inputs into faming and mining and shipping away the farm produce and minerals. However, this is changing since Concession assumed the status of an administrative centre.

4.5. Existing development and development plans for Nzvimbo DSC

Nzvimbo was designated as the District Service Centre (DSC) in the early 1980s, soon after independence, and some infrastructure was put in place to enhance its status. Today it is just a sub office, after Concession became the headquarters of the RDC. Nzvimbo has a balanced provision of residential, commercial, industrial, and institutional stands. However, expansion of the centre seems to have resumed after slowing down in the past. Several homesteads have been incorporated into the centre. Plans are on the way to expand it by 250 stands. Some inhabitants of communal land have let second or third principal homesteads develop on their plots. There is a road by-pass to the east of the settlement from Glendale to Muzarabani, which took away passing by traffic and business.

4.6. Existing development and development plans for Kanhukamwe Business Centre

At Kanhukamwe Business Centre (BC), those displaced by the expansion of the business centre and the setting up of the irrigation scheme were allocated irrigable land. Further residential expansion of the Kanhukamwe BC may leave displaced people without such compensation. Part of the reason why Kanhukamwe BC is mostly residential development is because of the existence of Rosa service centre about 3 km east on the highway from Glendale. There is demand for land for the establishment of residential areas around Glendale.

4.7. Forms of displacement at the selected urban centres

Communal farmers in Nzvimbo area and Kanhukamwe area were affected directly and indirectly by Statutory Instrument 379 of 1982 which gazetted urban centres in communal lands. Homesteads and fields were incorporated into the DSC and BC as the boundaries of these settlements were outlined. The villagers were then told that the open fields had become council land to be planned for residential, commercial and industrial land uses. Over time, the Mazowe RDC has been extending the centres to accommodate applicants on the housing waiting list. Because communal land is vested in the President and occupants are not owners of the land, it has been easy to take the villagers' open fields for settlement expansion.

Nzvimbo had a by-pass created for the road from Glendale to Muzarabani. The road encouraged further expansion eastward of the settlement incorporating more villagers into Nzvimbo DSC. The road took away passers-by business and left people in the communal land between the by-pass and the growing settlement to worry about their future. An entrepreneur has put up a petrol-filling station at the junction of the by-pass and a new road into the settlement, which can be seen as a sign that the settlement development is being pulled toward the by-pass. In other places, like Dema in Seke, settlements have jumped to the other side of the by-pass leading to more displacements.

Kanhukamwe communal area has also been affected by the establishment of an irrigation scheme east of the BC. The residential estate is expanding west and north-west of the commercial part of the BC. The displacement of villagers has been at two levels, first to pave way for the irrigation scheme and next to accommodate the layout plan for a residential estate. The urban settlement has been taken right to the boundary fence of the homesteads in the communal lands, thereby putting pressure on the homesteads that are still outside the Kanhukamwe BC boundary.

The land reform programme also resulted in the displacement of commercial farmers in line with the Land Acquisition Act. Farms were acquired by government after designation. The Ministry of Lands holds these farms on behalf of government in Mazowe and Concession. The acquisition process is not yet complete on a number of the farms. Mazowe RDC cannot effectively plan on peri-urban farms because they have become state land under the administration of the Ministry of Lands. The farmers have left the farms and some of the farm workers have also left. Other farm workers continue to stay on the farms and find other means to survive.

Within the vicinity of Mazowe, one of the farms has been taken over by a bank. Through its estates section, municipal infrastructure is being put in place. Former farm workers are to find their way out. Some still reside on the farm on those areas where the infrastructure is not yet fully developed. The displacement of farm workers has resulted from an estate development company taking over the management of the land and its transition into urban settlement.

There are cases where people have occupied pieces of land illegally. When council or the owner takes steps to develop the piece of land through subdivision into urban settlement, these people who were not supposed to be there in the first place are displaced and they have to be catered for. There are cases where councils register these people who have settled illegally and ask them to pay rates and levies. However, when development is carried out later, these people are not recognised by council and are removed from the place.

There is also displacement which is hidden. After the boundaries of an urban centre have expanded and the land is put under urban development, farmers close to the urban centre reduce farming activity as a risk-exposure reduction strategy. Indirectly, some farm workers find themselves without employment and they have to move out.

5. Compensation for displacement

5.1. Commercial farmers

Private farm owners, whose land was taken over by central government, e.g. as part of the land reform, will be compensated through the Land Acquisition Act, which has been the position of the government. Some farmers who were displaced due to the acquisition process took their own initiative to find farms to rent and continue farming, e.g. some are growing maize or soya beans on rented farms in the Mazowe Valley.

5.2. Farm workers

There has generally been no compensation or support for displaced farm workers who lived on the farms. A few lucky ones were given transport by the farm owners to carry their belongings to new places of residence. For those who are still on the farms that are being developed as urban settlements, the future is not clear. Some suggest they should be given a stand on these subdivided farms as recognition for their service, especially in the Mazowe and Concession area. Some farm workers who were earlier displaced have found a new employer on the same farm that they had been asked to leave at an earlier period. Due to the lack of compensation or relocation measures, displaced farm workers have been left to fend for themselves and depend on their survival skills. Some of the former farm workers became involved in gold panning. One of the farm workers in Mazowe Valley pointed out that some farmers from Zimbabwe who moved to Zambia have recruited experienced farm workers that they once worked with, which opened an avenue for a few displaced farm workers to earn a living.

5.3. Development companies

Land development companies are generally not interested in the history of the land. Real estate development is their focus. The displaced on the land under development are expected to approach Mazowe RDC for help.

5.4. Council (RDC)

The Ministry of Lands is holding on to gazetted farms in Mazowe urban and within the vicinity of Mazowe Dam. Mazowe RDC expects these to be handed over to them so that they have full control in planning the expansion of Mazowe urban settlement and in handling part of the compensation issue. The RDC seems to be ready to accept the farms and work out compensation issues with the displaced farmers based on the Regional, Town and Country Planning Act, Land Acquisition Act and Rural District Councils Act. However, there are more sticking issues beyond the farm owners, e.g. the farm workers and related dependants who have been displaced as well. These vulnerable farm workers need help and support, which seems to not be on the table.

5.5. Central government

The Government of Zimbabwe through the Ministry of Lands and Ministry of Local Government maintains that the displaced land owners around Mazowe urban and Concession urban will be compensated. Compensation for the residents of communal lands displaced at Nzvimbo and Kanhukamwe is the responsibility of Mazowe RDC. The Mashonaland Central Provincial Lands Committee encourages those who have been displaced to register with the lands committee and be on the waiting list for land allocation when plots are made available.

5.6. Villagers (*Nzvimbo and Kanhukamwe*)

When the irrigation scheme was established at Kanhukamwe area, the village was reorganised. The affected were allocated rain-fed land within a planned village with much smaller pieces of land than before. This was compensated by an allocation of an acre of irrigated land that allows all year round farming. Market gardening was encouraged and agricultural extension officers were assigned to the irrigation scheme. In the process some of the land was set aside for Kanhukamwe BC expansion. In having this comprehensive plan, compensation issues were addressed at least through guaranteed irrigation fed farming. Grazing land was reduced but enough was left to keep animals for draught power. The residential component of the BC is there to cater for the younger generation of residents who need their own place of residence. Also the settlement density of the surrounding villages is intensifying, due to headmen and village heads allowing people to settle in the area. In the near future there will be no land left.

Nzvimbo, the other communal land settlement, is different from Kanhukamwe. Once the headquarters of Chiweshe District Council, it qualified to be designated as the DSC. In the same vein it appeared in the 1982 prescription regulations as an area to be turned urban. In subdividing the communal land to create a layout plan, the rural homesteads were incorporated into the layout and villagers automatically owned the stands hosting their homesteads. The other stands from the open fields were allocated to those on the housing waiting list who bought them from council. The villagers, whose fields were taken over for urban development, were left to stay on the stand on which their homestead was built and no payment was made for the intrinsic value of the land they lost, in accordance with the Communal Land Act. However, compensation was made through allocating the affected villagers market stalls to conduct business to improve livelihoods, although not all of them received such. Although the villagers were not physically displaced, they became economically displaced, since they lost their fields and grazing areas and therefore the means of their agro-based livelihoods. The allocation of market stalls was intended to mitigate this kind of displacement.

Compensation has become a hot issue as these centres expand and people are more and more aware of their rights. They no longer part with their fields easily. Some of the villagers were asked to register with the lands committee so that they can be allocated farming land elsewhere as a replacement for the forfeited communal land. Unfortunately, land is finite so it is becoming increasingly difficult to find alternative land. On the other hand, the waiting list is growing.

5.7. Constraints on compensation in Mazowe

One of the major constraints is lack of financial resources which forces authorities to skirt the compensation issue or take long to avail compensation, e.g. the Mazowe urban case and the Nzvimbo DSC case. Local authorities and central government need adequate resources to carry out such processes. Land availability is becoming scarce, which makes it difficult to offer alternative land to the displaced across all the four settlements under discussion. To convince someone to part with his/her land and move somewhere else or to accept the compensation on offer needs skilled negotiators, who at times are not available. Ineffective development controls result in operation *garawadya* where an exploitation of a weakness in the system leads to new homesteads appearing on open communal land designated for development under the RDC – making it difficult to manage settlement expansion.

Development-induced displacements are happening where local authorities realign the demarcation of the boundaries of a district service centre, rural service centre or business centre. Due to fears of being displaced without fair compensation, people with homesteads around the new boundaries often take it upon themselves to subdivide their land and sell the plots/stands ahead of the local authority (one may say to pre-empt future developments) in order to also benefit from 'one's land'. In the process, the planned settlement expansion provokes a set of events which becomes increasingly difficult to control by the local authorities, who are then facing an influx of illegal settlers around urban centres which they struggle to evict, thereby further complicating the compensation issue.

5.8. Tangible cultural heritage

There are places, though not many, which deserve consideration as cultural heritage to be protected and preserved. There are the areas of indigenous trees forming forests in the Concession and Mazowe areas. Developers intending to promote Mazowe Valley as a tourist centre argue that the only way forward is to protect the woodlands as much as possible. The trees are a heritage that is difficult to compensate. The sacred places cannot be moved. Traditional ceremonies should be allowed to continue to take place in those areas even after displacement, as a way to pacify the 'spirits'. A possible route of compensation is to maintain, preserve and protect the sites permanently.

Cemeteries and graves are found in all of the four study areas. At Kanhukamwe BC the main issue were graves within the dam site. Chief Negomo had to perform a ritual to dig out the remains of the dead and rebury them. They also performed rituals to cover those whose graves may not have been identified to rest in peace under the water. Compensation was in the form of paying for the rituals and reburials to happen, which was supported by the authorities. At Kanhukamwe and Nzvimbo new graveyards were established to cater for the closed cemeteries and create order. Some of the graves were left undisturbed within the stands in which they are found. In this case, compensation claims did not arise as far as the council is concerned. The same applies to Mazowe urban and Concession where some land developers pay for the rituals to remove the graves, if they conclude it is necessary to do so.

Council and developers or investors are in agreement that the game park nearby Mazowe urban, with famous wildlife species like rhino, giraffe and buffalo, should be left untouched to support the development of tourism infrastructure in the area. It is hoped that some of the farm workers who have been displaced may get jobs in the expanding tourism industry. In this case the tangible heritage is protected.

6. Conclusion

This chapter outlined the laws and regulations that are used in managing urban expansions and dealing with displacement and compensation issues from a spatial planning perspective. The level of urban expansion in the four centres studied has been demonstrated through unpacking the proposed developments. The different categories of people who were displaced were analysed and the form of compensation made available to them described. Urbanisation is taking place and land demands are high. For land to be made available, it has to be purchased or if compulsorily acquired then properly compensated for. Mazowe RDC is in a difficult position as it finds itself with peri-urban development which is on land under central government in some cases or private developers in other cases. The issue of compensation for the people being displaced due to urban development has not been handled in a systematic manner and varies from centre to centre. Even where future displacements are to take place, to date no plans are being put in place to handle compensation issues fairly. Not enough attention is being paid to tangible cultural heritage, although in some cases it is dealt with as part of the compensation process, e.g. Kanhukamwe. If Mazowe urban expansion takes place, there are serious challenges in terms of protection and compensation of tangible cultural heritage that need to be addressed.

6.1. Lessons from Mazowe district

- Scarcity of land availability demands re-strategizing on how compensation can be handled.
- Preservation of tangible cultural heritage needs further probing followed by policy formulation.
- The use of information and communication technology (ICT) can help in monitoring development and dealing with the development of illegal settlements.
- Mazowe Valley needs a comprehensive spatial plan.
- Development plans need to include the issue of displacement and compensation and respective budgets need to avail adequate resources.

6.2. Strategies

- Mazowe District has a lot of mines. Mazowe RDC set up its 'Community Share Ownership Trust' a few years ago, but to date only a few thousand dollars have been realised to start implementing community projects in the district. If the community trust funds were to be collected, the funds would go a long way in addressing compensation issues and social infrastructure development to improve the welfare of the people.
- The grey area of who is in charge of peri-urban farms needs resolving.
- The welfare of those who are being displaced can be linked to some of the economic activities that are being mooted. The RDC should see how the displaced can be prepared to learn new skills in line with proposed developments.
- The rich Mazowe agricultural land needs protection to avoid food shortage problems. Current layout plans are too generous and exacerbate urban sprawl. Vertical development in urban areas could be a feasible option thus mitigating displacement and compensation issues.
- Promote irrigation farming to accommodate more people on agricultural land.
- Allocation of land for dry land farming to the displaced should take into consideration farming skills and knowledge.
- Where possible, the displaced should be allocated a stand in the residential area to at least have basic shelter and the opportunity to plan a life from there.
- Put future-oriented spatial plans in place and follow them religiously.
- Further look into the issue of tangible cultural heritage, take stock of all assets and account for them when planning for development.

References

Ashworth, G. J., B. J. Graham and J. E. Tunbridge (2007). *Pluralising Pasts: Heritage, Identity and Place in Multicultural Societies.* London: Pluto Press.

Bidandi, F. (2018). "The Dynamics of Urbanisation in Kampala, Uganda: Towards a Possible Urban Policy Framework", University of the

Norwegian Refugee Centre.

Government of Zimbabwe (2002). Rural District Councils Act, Chapter 29:13. Harare: Government Printer.

—— (2002a). Communal Land Act, Chapter 20:04. Harare: Government Printer.

—— (2002b). Land Acquisition Act, Chapter 20:10. Harare: Government Printer.

—— (1996). Urban Councils Act, Chapter 29:15. Harare: Government Printer.

—— (1996a). Regional, Town and Country Planning Act, Chapter 29:12. Harare: Government Printer.

—— (1982). Statutory Instrument 379 of 1982. Harare: Government Printer.

Jonga, W. and K. Munzwa, K. (2010). "Urban Development in Zimbabwe: A Human Settlement Perspective", Theoretical and Empirical Researches in Urban Management. Theoretical and Empirical Researches in Urban Management, 5(14), pp.120-146.

Mbiba, B. (2017) "On the Periphery: Missing Urbanization in Zimbabwe", Africa Research Institute.

Ukoje, E. (2016). "Impacts of Rapid Urbanisation in the Urban Fringe of Lakoja, Nigeria", Journal of Geography and Regional Planning, 9(10), pp.185-194.

Vecco, M. (2010). "A Definition of Cultural Heritage: From the Tangible to the Intangible", Journal of Cultural Heritage, 11(3), pp.321-324.

Zimbabwe National Statistical Agency (2015). Population Projection Thematic Report. Harare: Government Printer.

—— (2013). Zimbabwe Census 2012 Report. Harare: Government Printer.

8

Challenges to Relocation and Compensation of Rural Communities Displaced by Development Projects: Case Studies from the Midlands Province

Christof Schmidt & Shadreck Vengesai

1. Introduction

1.1. Background and problem

Across the globe and particularly in developing countries, local communities face risks of being displaced by public and private infrastructure and development projects, such as dam and road constructions, urbanisation and urban expansion, commercial farming and forestry, or mineral exploration and mining. In China, 70 million people were displaced between 1950 and 2000, while 50 million people were affected in India. A study carried out by the World Bank shows that in the majority of cases of development-induced displacements, standards of living have declined and poverty increased among the affected people (Tripathi 2017). Local communities residing in areas earmarked for developments become victims of economic, social and cultural disruptions, as they are uprooted from their ancestral homes and the environment they often have built strong attachments to, owing to generations of occupation. Economic, social and cultural systems are lost in the process, especially if there are no concerted efforts and programmes to compensate the affected people and to rehabilitate their livelihoods.

Africa has seen many cases of such displacements in the past. For example, between 20,000 and 30,000 people were displaced for a gold mine in the Ghanaian region of Tarkwa, 160,000 people lost their homes due to a pipeline project in South Sudan, and 50,000 Maasai people were displaced in the creation of the Serengeti National Park (Terminski 2018, p.18). Zimbabwe has its own long history of displacements linked to destructive colonial settlement policies resulting in the displacement of black people residing in areas reserved for white settlers, as well as the construction of the Kariba Dam which displaced an estimated 57,000 people and had long-lasting negative effects on the affected Tonga people. Some countries of the Southern African Development Community (SADC) like Mozambique have recently tried to address the issue by crafting comprehensive regulations for relocation and resettlement processes (CCJP 2014, Annex 6.6).

In post-independence Zimbabwe, dam constructions and mining have been major causes of development-induced involuntary human mobility. A survey conducted by the Zimbabwe Vulnerability Assessment Committee indicates that 8% of the population have been affected by displacements between 2000 and 2007.[1] The Tugwi-Mukosi Dam construction, which was intended to provide irrigation and electricity to communities in the semi-arid Masvingo Province, displaced approximately 2,000 households[2] and resulted in untold suffering of thousands of people who were left homeless, landless and destitute (HRW 2015). The current Mines and Mineral Act gives mining precedence over agriculture (SMAIAS 2018, p.4) and especially in Manicaland Province local communities have been negatively affected by mining-induced displacements, e.g. for diamond mining in Chiadzwa which displaced 600 households (Madebwe et al 2011). In addition, the bio-ethanol plant in Chisumbanje displaced approximately 1,600 households in Manicaland (Thondhlana 2014, p.8). The burden of the costs for rehabilitating the livelihoods of the affected people was disproportionately borne by the communities themselves.

Furthermore, some areas in Zimbabwe have witnessed rapid urbanisation in the past 30 years. Expansion of towns, growth points and rural service centres has resulted in displacement and relocation of local communities who are expected to cede land to pave way for urban and rural development. Across the country, such processes have triggered

---

1 17% of the respondents from 30 districts have relocated since 2000 and almost half of them had been "asked to move" (IDMC 2008, p.41).
2 "$1.5 million for Tokwe Mukosi dam flood victims", *Newsday*, 29 May 2019.

local conflicts between the authorities and communities occupying land earmarked for urban and rural development. It has been the experience of the Centre for Conflict Management and Transformation (CCMT) that these conflicts are often structural and related to weaknesses in the land tenure systems and compensation policies, which contribute to situations in which communities resist relocations because they feel unfairly treated and insufficiently compensated.

1.2. Research background and purpose

Since 2013, CCMT has been conducting interventions to transform conflicts between local authorities and communities on relocation and compensation issues resulting from development projects in the Midlands Province. During these interventions, stakeholders realised that some aspects of these conflicts are structural and need to be addressed by reforming policies and harmonizing the different approaches applied by local authorities.

In 2017, CCMT in cooperation with the Provincial Administrator's office supported local authorities from the eight rural districts of the province in jointly developing recommendations and guidelines that intend to minimise displacement and relocation conflicts by facilitating mutual agreements and responsiveness to the concerns and human needs of the affected communities, which participated in the process. This research is part of the efforts to encourage dialogue and interrogation of policies and legislation in and beyond the Midlands Province.

The primary goal of this chapter is to highlight policy gaps and practical challenges that contribute to the escalation of conflicts between communities and local authorities in cases where communities have to cede rural land for development purposes. The secondary goal is to analyse the strengths and weaknesses of different approaches towards relocation and compensation that have been applied in practice by the authorities. The research was guided by the following questions:

- What are the rights of smallholder farmers and rural communities in terms of relocation and compensation according to the legislation and policy framework in Zimbabwe?
- Are these rights and current policies sufficient in terms of mitigating potential negative effects of relocations on the livelihoods and development of the affected communities?
- Which approaches are applied in practice by the responsible

authorities when they relocate and compensate rural communities?
- What are the specific conflict issues and challenges emerging in the relocation process?
- How does relocation impact on the affected communities and how could such processes and compensation packages be improved from their perspective?

Preliminary desk research revealed that there have been several studies about displacements caused by political conflicts, dams and mining in Zimbabwe. However, only very few studies focus on recent cases that occurred in the context of other infrastructure development projects, such as urban expansions. Even fewer studies look beyond the immediate effects of physical relocation and explore the medium- and long-term impact, as well as the positive and negative aspects of the resettlement and compensation approaches applied by the authorities in terms of restoring the livelihoods and socio-economic development of affected communities.

This chapter intends to contribute towards closing this gap by presenting findings on the approaches and results of specific relocation cases that occurred in the context of development projects in the Midlands Province. For the purpose of this research, three cases were examined and analysed in terms of critical aspects, such as consultations, resettlement, compensation, and rehabilitation. By linking the findings to provisions and gaps in the Zimbabwean legislation and policy framework on relocation and compensation of rural communities, this chapter aims to provide relevant information for policy dialogues at local, provincial and national levels.

1.3. Research methodology

For the purpose of this research, best practices were identified by reviewing secondary literature on displacements, relocations and compensation of local communities in and beyond Zimbabwe. In addition, three distinct cases in the Midlands Province were identified in which communities have been relocated due to development projects. The three cases occurred in different decades (1998, 2002, 2013) and districts (Mberengwa, Shurugwi, Zvishavane) and involved different approaches and stakeholders. The cases were identified and selected in cooperation with Mberengwa Rural District Council, Tongogara Rural District Council and Runde Rural District Council.

The three cases affected a total of 105 households with approximately 600 people, of which a sample of 52 households with one respondent from each household was interviewed using a structured questionnaire (14 out of 35 households from Mberengwa, 20 out of 30 households in Zvishavane, 18 out of 40 households in Shurugwi). Affected community members were also asked to map their access to public facilities, services and resources within a distance of 15 kilometres and to compare the situation before and after the relocation.[3]

The collected data was triangulated through facilitating semi-structured focus group discussions with community members and conducting key informant interviews with district development coordinators, chief executive officers, executive officers planning/engineering/technical services, and councillors for the three councils. The data was further validated and consolidated through reviewing relevant documents provided by key informants and information gathered from local conflict interventions facilitated by CCMT.

1.4. Definition of key terms

- *Local authorities* are elected and appointed representatives of certain areas that form a Rural District Council, as well as local government officials for the district and provincial administration.

- *Responsible authorities* for relocation and compensation are all stakeholders responsible for the planning and implementation of such processes, e.g. the local authorities, the Ministry of Local Government, the Ministry of Lands, Agriculture and Rural Resettlement, and in some cases state-owned enterprises or private sector stakeholders, such as mining companies and land developers.

- *Displacement* refers to involuntary or forced human mobility from the habitual homeland. Even if affected people are not physically displaced, they may still be economically displaced as a result of

---

3   With regards to social facilities and infrastructure, the respondents considered schools, clinics, business centres and roads. Boreholes, irrigable land, community projects, shared fields, and grazing land were amongst the facilities classified as community developments and commons. The respondents also rated the functionality of critical public services and institutions, such as agricultural extension services, veterinary services, traditional leadership, and village and ward development committees. Another crucial aspect was the state of the environment and access to natural resources like watershed areas and forests. Some community members also emphasized heritage and cultural sites, e.g. sacred places, grave sites or other culturally or religiously relevant facilities.

the development project affecting their environment, livelihoods or socio-economic rights.
- *Relocation* or *resettlement* refers to pre-planned physical relocation, including appropriate support mechanisms which facilitate the process.
- *Compensation* refers to financial payments, material replacements or any other form of support received by the affected people in order to compensate them for any damages or losses they reasonably incurred due to the process of displacement or relocation. Compensation is guided by the principle of equivalence: affected people should be neither enriched nor impoverished due to the process. However, an improvement of their situation is usually desirable.
- *Rehabilitation* goes beyond physical relocation and refers to integrated programmes and measures designed to mitigate or reverse the risks and negative effects of relocation on livelihoods and socio-economic development in a sustainable manner.
- *Land tenure* refers to the relationships, rights and regulations that define ownership, access, use, control, and transfer of land. Land tenure systems determine who can use which resources for how long and under what conditions.
- *Growth points* are settlements earmarked for economic and physical development. Growth points were created by the Government of Zimbabwe to redress imbalances in the nature of the colonial economy by providing focal points for local investment in neglected rural areas. By decentralizing investment, the government tries to develop services, employment, markets, and primary processing within rural areas in order to curb rural-urban migration.

2. Land tenure and compensation of rural communities

2.1. Land tenure systems in Zimbabwe

Zimbabwe has complex and diverse settlement patterns, land tenure systems and compensation regulations, which are the result of colonisation and the various efforts after independence to redress colonial inequalities. During colonial times, the most arable land regions I-III were reserved for white settlers, who obtained freehold titles that provided ownership of agricultural land in perpetuity and could only be traded with other white settlers. Black settlers could also own agricultural land, but were restricted to designated "Native Purchase Areas" which were often located in remote areas with land of poorer quality (Scoones 2017).

The majority of black farmers resided in overcrowded and overused 'Tribal Trust Lands' which were predominantly located in region V, administered on behalf of the indigenous population, and specifically reserved for 'native' occupation and usage. Land parcels were allocated internally by traditional leaders according to local customs, although white native commissioners were ultimately responsible for land allocation to Africans. The remaining land in Zimbabwe was designated national land for wildlife reserves, which would later become national parks.

After independence in 1980, every Zimbabwean was given the right to purchase agricultural land in any region with the important exception of 'Communal Land' and 'Resettlement Areas'. The former 'Tribal Trust Lands' were transformed into state land vested in the President of Zimbabwe. In practice, the traditional leaders retained their role in allocating parcels to local residents who were collectively permitted to occupy and use state land designated as communal land for residential and agricultural purposes. In addition, the government started acquiring farms owned by white settlers, which were transformed into state land designated for resettlement of mainly small-scale farmers (Gonese et al 2002, pp.10-12). Communal lands were increasingly affected by environmental degradation and residents and returning refugees from the liberation war were given the opportunity to apply for resettlement. Resettlement land could not be owned or purchased and initially parcels were allocated customarily as in communal lands, but increasingly settlers obtained open ended settlement permits which gave individuals or groups the right to occupy and use certain parcels allocated by the local authorities.

In the early 2000s, Zimbabwe embarked on a more far-reaching land reform and the government undertook compulsory acquisition of land owned by white farmers without compensation for the land. As a result, the system of freehold titles for agricultural land was largely abandoned and became increasingly restricted to non-agricultural land, while most agricultural land became state land. The expropriated land was subdivided and classified as either A1 farms for the resettlement of small-scale farmers or A2 farms for medium- to large-scale commercial farming. The government invited all interested and qualified Zimbabweans to apply for resettlement and issued temporary offer letters for occupation of designated

A2 or A1 farms. Subsequently, A1 settlers or groups could obtain indefinite settlement permits for occupation and usage from the Ministry of Lands and Rural Resettlement. In addition, the government introduced regulated 99-year leaseholds for A2 farmers using allocated state land for commercial agriculture on a larger scale.

Since the fast track land reform, the public discourse about land tenure, resettlement and compensation in Zimbabwe has been dominated by issues related to the compensation of evicted white farmers and the regulation of 99-year leases in order to improve security of land tenure for medium- to large-scale commercial farms. Despite the crucial role of rural communities and smallholder farmers for the economic, social and cultural development in Zimbabwe, there has not been sufficient attention and action to address similar challenges they are facing.

Local communities usually face potential displacement if the authorities decide to change the use of state land that had been designated for occupation by rural communities in order to pave way for development projects. While this often seems a rather technical problem of land use management from the perspective of the authorities, the communities deal with severe risks in terms of their livelihoods and development. They often try to resist and end up in conflict with the authorities, if they feel they are not fairly treated and adequately compensated for their losses. For the purpose of this research, it is critical to have a more detailed look at the rights of smallholders and rural communities in terms of land tenure, protection from arbitrary displacement and compensation for diminution of any such rights.

Residents of communal lands and resettlement areas have the right to occupy and use designated state land, although they have no ownership of the land. In order to protect the livelihoods and development of local communities, they enjoy the right to be compensated, if their rights to occupy and use the land are affected. However, weaknesses in the land tenure and land administration systems, gaps in the legislation and policies on compensation, as well as power imbalances in practice have resulted in cases in which communities have suffered significant losses when they had to cede land. Furthermore, relocation and compensation processes are not regulated by a harmonised policy framework. As a result, different authorities apply different approaches and at times impose inadequate or unsustainable compensation models.

2.2. Compensation of occupants in communal areas

Communal land is state land vested in the President of Zimbabwe. Local communities, regardless of their historical claims and how long they would have occupied the land, have no ownership but are permitted to occupy and use communal land, according to section 4 and 7 of the Communal Land Act. Section 12 of the Communal Land Act provides that if "any person is dispossessed of or suffers any diminution of his right to occupy or use any land", they shall be given the right to occupy or use alternative land and/or an agreement as to compensation shall be reached. If no alternative land is available and no agreement has been reached, Section V and VIII of the Land Acquisition Act shall apply.[4] The following relevant issues in terms of compensation are left open and at the discretion of the responsible authorities:

- Ensuring that the alternative land is equivalent and as adequate for the intended occupation and use as the previously held land;
- Improvements and disturbances to be considered for agreements on compensation;
- Ensuring that communities have similar access to social facilities, public infrastructure and services, commons and natural resources on alternative land.

According to the Manual for the Management of Urban Land (MoLG 2002), authorities intending to expand urban land into communal land have to reach an agreement on compensation with the affected communities. The agreement has to be submitted as an addendum to the application for excision of communal land and needs to be approved by the Ministry of Local Government. However, neither the Communal Land Act nor the Manual provide details on how such an agreement shall be reached and which areas of concern it is supposed to cover as a minimum requirement.

Although the occupants of communal land are already disadvantaged due to limited rights to the land, there are no provisions to ensure sufficient public notice, consultations, assessments or negotiations based on equal bargaining powers, which according to the Food and Agriculture Organization of the United Nations are critical aspects for reaching agreements on compensation (FAO 2008, p.42). The cases investigated

---

4 However, the application of the Land Acquisition Act is difficult in terms of compensation for such land, since communal land cannot be purchased and therefore has no official market value.

by this research show that local communities are usually not consulted in the development of compensation agreements and do not have access to professional advice or legal representation. Since the responsible authorities usually have an interest to keep compensation costs as low as possible, there is thus a considerable risk that 'agreements' may be imposed on local communities.

2.3. Compensation of occupants in Model A and A1 resettlement areas

Model A and A1 resettlement areas comprise of smallholder beneficiaries of the land reform programme. After independence, a *villagised Model A* was used which derived its design from communal lands. Model A was later modified into *villagised Model A1* which provides a 0.5 hectare residential plot, 5 hectares individual arable land holding and 25 to 60 hectares communal grazing land depending on the size of the community. In addition, a *self-contained Model A1* with 25 to 50 hectare was introduced, which was supposed to cater for all residential, arable and grazing requirements of each household, instead of reliance on communal allocation and provision of resources (Gonese et al 2002, p.23).

As is the case with communal land tenure, occupants do not own the land in resettlement areas. In terms of Statutory Instrument (SI) 53 of 2014 which regulates settlement permits, the land is retained by the state and settlers are to be issued with indefinite permits to reside on the land, cultivate it and graze livestock. However, according to section 20 the Minister of Lands has the authority to terminate or cancel permits at his sole discretion after giving three months' written notice. Although SI 53 of 2014 gives a right to claim compensation for improvements and crops growing on the allocated land, the following areas are of concern in terms of compensation:

- No obligation to provide alternative land or otherwise compensate for loss of land as main source of livelihood;
- No guidance on how, when and by whom assessments of improvements and crops are supposed to be carried out;
- Compensation is explicitly restricted to improvements and crops only, which leaves no flexibility for consideration of any other relevant losses incurred;
- Settlers may be dispossessed before receiving any compensation.

According to SI 53 of 2014, compensation agreed upon or determined must be paid not later than 180 days from the date when the government resumes possession of the allocated land that was subject to the permit, while the government reserves the right to resume possession within 90 days of the written notice. Although in default of agreements compensation shall be determined by arbitration, this does not only leave room for severe disruptions of livelihoods but also fails to ensure that actual compensation values have been assessed before taking repossession of the land.

In practice, the situation is further complicated because there is a backlog in issuing settlement permits and occupants often have no tenure document at all. In general, beneficiaries of resettlement schemes are more vulnerable than the occupants of communal lands. This is because they feel indebted to the benevolence of the government which availed them the land as part of its resettlement policy, while occupants of communal land often feel some sense of ownership or entitlement to the land and its surroundings owing to generations of occupation. As a result, occupants of communal land are more likely to oppose displacement and to claim bargaining power than occupants of resettlement areas when faced with displacement.

3. Relocation and compensation in practice: three cases in the Midlands Province

For the purpose of this research, three representative cases from different decades and districts have been selected which demonstrate different approaches to relocation and compensation with distinct strengths, weaknesses and results. The first case occurred in Mberengwa District between 1998 and 2000, when 35 households were relocated to pave way for Mataga Growth Point. A second sample was taken from Zvishavane District, where 30 households were moved in 2013 due to an expansion of Zvishavane Town which involved a land developer. The third case is related to the Unki platinum project by international mining group Anglo American, which required the relocation of 40 households from the proposed project site in Shurugwi District in 2002. In total, approximately 600 people were affected by these cases. The research focused on how the responsible authorities dealt with consultations, resettlement, compensation, and rehabilitation issues, as well as the impact on the affected communities and the appraisal of each aspect of the process by community members.

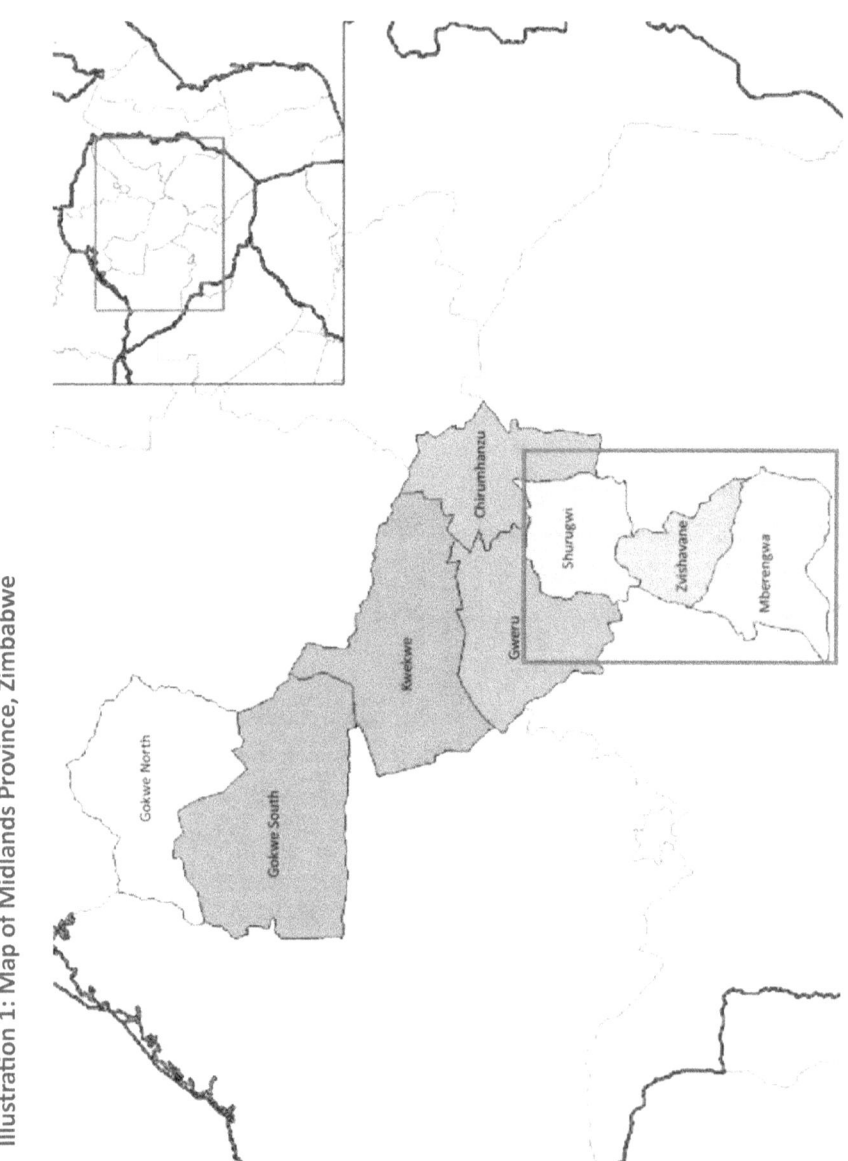

Illustration 1: Map of Midlands Province, Zimbabwe

Table 1: Information on selected cases

District	Year of re-location	Former location	Current location	Reason for re-location	Responsible authorities
(a) Mberengwa	1998-2000	Ward: 18 Village: Chipedza / Chagwiza	Ward: 36 Village: Bungwe Re-settlement I	Growth point expansion	Local authorities / Min. of Local Gov./ Min. of Lands
(b) Zvishavane	2013	Ward: 13 Village: Mabhula	Ward: 5 Village: 5 Mhondongori	Town expansion	Local authorities / Min. of Lands /Land developer
(c) Shurugwi	2002	Ward: 19 Village: 18 Chironde	Ward: 21 Village: 1 Reitfontein	Platinum mining	Local authorities / Min. of Lands / Mining company

3.1. Consultations and negotiations

Both the Communal Land Act and the Statutory Instrument (SI) 53 of 2014 encourage agreements between the authority requiring land and the affected communities. Agreements are usually reached through public consultations and negotiations between the responsible authorities and the affected communities or representatives of their choice. In the three cases at hand, the affected communities were informed by the responsible authorities about the relocation, but the terms of the resettlement and compensation packages were agreed upon without community participation. Two communities were not consulted in public meetings and only one community obtained a written agreement, however, only after they approached the Administrative Court.

The affected community in Mberengwa had first read in the newspaper about plans to expand the growth point and to relocate them from their communal land. Afterwards, the Mberengwa Rural District Council called for a meeting with community leaders and announced the relocation, but was met with resistance from the chief and community. They were told that it was against the law to stay on land earmarked for development and, subsequently, some community members started registering for resettlement out of fear of otherwise not being compensated. In 1998, the community became a beneficiary of a resettlement scheme launched by the President of Zimbabwe and most households moved until 2000, after they had been threatened with forced eviction and became afraid of farming operations being disrupted.

The affected community in Zvishavane consisted of people from different areas who had been resettled voluntarily in the context of land redistribution policies shortly after independence. In 2012, the residents encountered contractors in the resettlement area who intended to develop the land for urban settlement. The community was then relocated in 2013, less than a month after being informed by the District Administrator and the chief that the land they occupied had been placed under town jurisdiction and was already pegged. The community engaged a lawyer from Harare and demanded USD $7,000 compensation per household, replacement of houses and urban residential stands. They were relocated eventually, after they had been promised to receive adequate compensation and signed an agreement, which was kept by the lawyer.

In Shurugwi, Unki mine was involved in the relocation of a local community in 2002. The mining company approached the community a year in advance and the local District Administrator and Rural District Council conducted public meetings to inform the community about plans to relocate and compensate them. However, according to the affected community members the applied approach was more instructive than consultative and the responsible authorities did not negotiate terms with the community, although they had been promised to have a choice between different resettlement areas and that they would receive employment opportunities from the mining company. The community relocated after being told that if they do not move, they would have to go back to where they came from thus reminding them of being beneficiaries of previous resettlement programmes.

In the absence of mutual agreements, any aggrieved party has the right to approach the Administrative Court for remedy. With regards to resettlement areas, SI 53 of 2014 states that disputes may be resolved in terms of the Arbitration Act. In accordance with section 297(d) of the 2013 Constitution of Zimbabwe, disputes could also be presented to the Land Commission. However, 87% of the respondents in all three cases did not know their rights, which restricted their ability to demand fair negotiations

Figure 1: Community level of satisfaction with consultations and negotiations

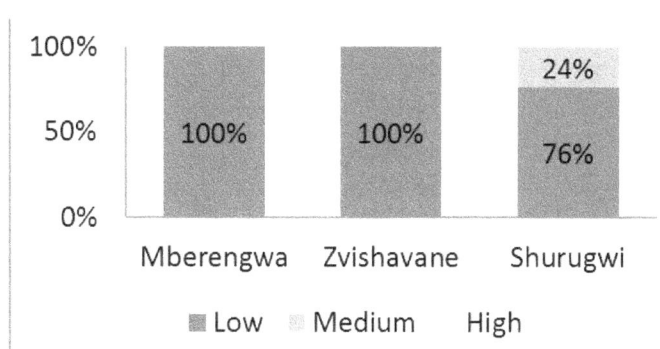

or to seek a court order. Nearly all respondents that were aware of their rights came from Shurugwi and reported that they had been informed about their rights during public consultations by the responsible authorities, although only 28% of them felt sufficiently informed.

The affected community members from Shurugwi would have preferred a more consultative approach and fair negotiations, but they decided not to take any actions against the relocation. In Zvishavane and Mberengwa, where communities had not been consulted and informed about their rights, the conflict escalated. The majority of community members in Zvishavane petitioned the local authorities and brought the case to the Administrative Court which ruled in their favour. Some of the affected community members from Mberengwa organised demonstrations and were arrested when they resisted the pegging of stands in their fields. While some households were relocated, others continued to resist moving, which resulted in a long-lasting conflict and standoff between the council and the community that was only resolved 20 years later through an intervention by CCMT.[5]

3.2. Resettlement on alternative land

Since agriculture is the main source of livelihoods for rural households in Zimbabwe, resettlement on adequate arable alternative land suitable for agricultural production becomes a critical aspect of relocation, unless access to other sustainable sources of livelihoods can be offered. The communities in Mberengwa and Zvishavane, which were relocated to pave way for urban development, ultimately benefitted from the resettlement in terms of being allocated better land than they had occupied before the relocation.

The affected households in Mberengwa received larger pieces of land with better soil quality. As residents of communal land, all respondents had occupied less than 5 hectares and the majority less than 2 hectares of land, but they were resettled on land ranging from 6 to 10 hectares. In Zvishavane, each household was allocated between 6 and 15 hectares of land. Although the majority of households had occupied up to 20 hectares before the relocation, the new location offered more arable land, good rainfall patterns and better soil quality, trees and perennial crops.

In contrast, the community in Shurugwi, which had to cede their land to a mining company, bemoaned that they had received smaller plots with less fertile soils, trees and perennial crops. 76% of the respondents previously had occupied 6 to 10 hectares, but only received 3 to 5 hectares. The affected community members reported that they used to harvest enough for their own consumption and surplus for sale, but at their new location they cannot even produce enough for themselves.

Figure 2: Community appraisal of land size, soil quality and trees/perennial crops after the relocation

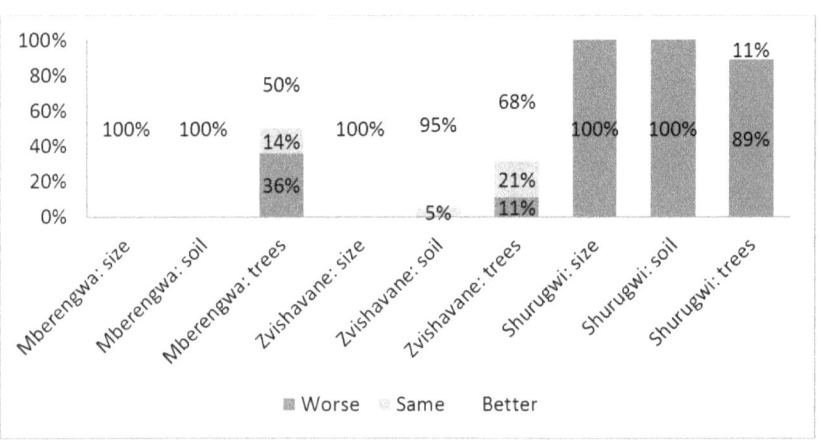

Despite being affected by involuntary relocation, in two out of the three cases the communities are not benefiting from improved security of their land tenure and receiving tenure documents. In Mberengwa, the households that previously had occupied communal land received settlement permits which they, however, had to obtain without assistance and at their own costs. The affected households in Zvishavane have not received any registration documents for their new land, although they used to have settlement permits for the land they had occupied before the relocation.

The households in Shurugwi have received offer letters which have not yet been replaced with indefinite settlement permits in line with Statutory Instrument 53 of 2014.

Table 2: Type and registration of former and current land

Case	Type and registration of previously occupied land	Type and registration of currently occupied land	Waiving of registration fees?
Mberengwa	Communal land / Not registered	Resettlement area / Settlement permit	Paid for permit
Zvishavane	Resettlement area / Settlement permit	Resettlement area / Not registered	-
Shurugwi	Resettlement area / Not registered	Resettlement area / Offer letter	-

The very different experiences of the communities in Zvishavane and Shurugwi in terms of land allocation are reflected in opposite development of livelihoods. In Shurugwi, the community lost access to artisanal mining and was resettled on less adequate land which resulted in deteriorated livelihoods for the vast majority of affected households. In contrast, a majority of affected community members in Zvishavane felt their livelihoods have improved, because they received more productive land and are harvesting better yields than in the area from which they were relocated. Despite having been allocated better land, the majority of the households affected by the case in Mberengwa reported deterioration of livelihoods since their relocation in the late 1990s and early 2000s.

Figure 3: Community appraisal of livelihood development after the relocation

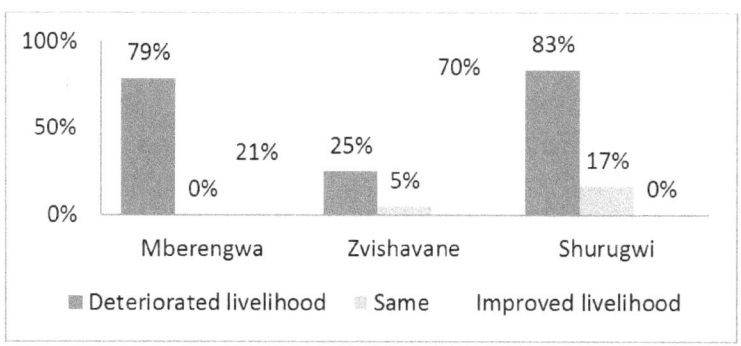

3.3. Compensation for improvements and disturbances

Statutory Instrument (SI) 53 of 2014, the Land Acquisition Act and the

Manual for the Management of Urban Land stipulate that occupants of resettlement areas and communal land that lose the land they occupy shall be compensated for improvements on such land. In addition, SI 53 of 2014 in section 20(1)(a) provides the right to be compensated for "any crops growing on the allocated land on the day of the cancellation or termination of the permit". Compensation, whether financial payments, material support or replacement of structures, is usually determined by an assessment or valuation of the immovable assets and any other damages the affected households reasonably incur due to the displacement. However, only in two of the three investigated cases valuations were carried out to establish compensation values.

In Mberengwa, the Regional Valuations Officer for the Matabeleland Region conducted assessments in October 1999 and submitted a valuation report to Mberengwa Rural District Council in November. The valuation was done on a "depreciated replacement cost basis" of existing structures and also took into consideration fruit trees, kraals and salvage values, but excluded the value of land which was state land. In addition, a disturbance allowance of 20% of the replacement costs was included. However, the valuation was not conducted in a consultative manner and took place after some households had already been resettled. Most community members were unaware of the assessment and the valuation methods applied. They felt they should have been given an opportunity to provide their own estimations and submissions to the valuator for further consideration. Some also raised concerns about possible conflicts of interest, since the valuation was conducted by a government official.

A similar assessment was commissioned by the local authorities and mining company in Shurugwi, where 11% of the respondents from the affected community reported that they also produced their own written submissions, which, however, were not considered. The exact process and valuation methods applied are not known because there was no documentation available. In Zvishavane, the authorities did not carry out any assessment of compensation values, which became apparent when the community took legal action against the relocation process. As a result, the Administrative Court estimated a flat fee and ruled that each household was entitled to USD $7,000 compensation as demanded by the community.

Although the valuation assessment in Mberengwa was comprehensive and determined financial compensation for improvements and disturbances, the affected community members ended up in a dire situation without access to housing because they were relocated without having received any compensation yet. The resultant crisis is evidenced by a letter written from the Midlands Provincial Administrator dated 15 January 2001 to Mberengwa Rural District Council, wherein he raised his concern over the continuous delay of the payment of compensation which left the affected community "desperate for accommodation".

A different approach was taken in the cases in Zvishavane and Shurugwi, where the involved land developer and mining company constructed identical houses for the relocated communities. In Shurugwi, the relocated people were housed in temporary shelters until the construction was finished. However, the affected communities in both districts expressed concerns over the size and quality of the houses. In the case of Zvishavane, some of the affected people reportedly used to have houses two times bigger than the ones they received. They deemed the new houses inadequate in terms of replacing the buildings they lost and not suitable for a rural setup. The newly constructed houses were also of worse quality and had cracks all over, which indicates that they were constructed hurriedly and without sufficient resources allocated for the construction.

Illustration 2: Houses constructed for community in Zvishavane (crack on top of the wall on the right side)

Before the relocation, most households in the affected areas owned three or more buildings for accommodation, sanitation and storage. In addition, most of them had erected demarcation and fencing and arranged drainage and access routes. In Zvishavane and Shurugwi, community members had irrigable land and the homesteads in Shurugwi were connected to the electrical grid. Despite the assessments that had been carried out in Shurugwi, the new houses were not comparable to the previously owned ones, but the responsible authorities ignored complaints about the size and quality of the buildings they had constructed. One of the affected community members from Shurugwi described the houses as a health hazard and remarked that "...the word 'replacement' loses its meaning when what is lost is not comparable to what is being offered, especially when what is offered is less than what was lost".

Figure 4: Community level of satisfaction with compensation for buildings and other improvements

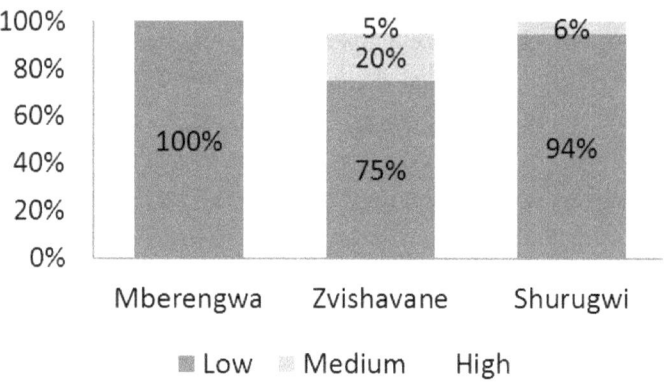

In all three cases, the relocation process resulted in disruptions and disturbance of livelihoods which particularly affected vulnerable groups. The relocated community members had to clear and cultivate the new land and transport movable household assets to the new location. 88% of all respondents reported that they lost crops, livestock or earnings due to the process. Although the affected households in Mberengwa and Zvishavane had been allocated better land, they experienced a very difficult first year. The community in Zvishavane was relocated amidst heavy floods and did not get any support in clearing and cultivating the new land, which was covered by a huge forest. 36% of the respondents from Mberengwa were assisted in tilling the land, but the remaining households did not receive any support either. In contrast, the affected community in Shurugwi was provided agricultural inputs (seeds and fertiliser) and a group orchard to start up their agricultural activities in the new area.

In Shurugwi and Mberengwa, the responsible authorities also supported the affected community members by providing trucks for moving their belongings to the new settlement. Instead of receiving transport, the affected households in Zvishavane were given an allowance of USD $90 each to transfer their cattle for a distance of 72 kilometres. However, the amount was reported to be insufficient because each household owned between eight and fourteen cattle, which they ended up walking for the whole distance with some livestock perishing along the way.

Figure 5: Community level of satisfaction with compensation for disruptions and disturbances

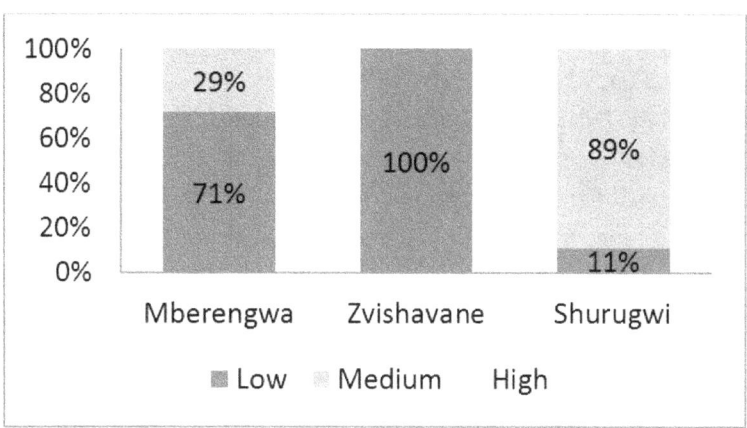

Table 3: Payment and amount of financial compensation per household

Mberengwa	USD $40 (payment in Zimbabwean Dollar, estimation of current value based on the price of a bag of wheat)	Cheque (4 years later)
Zvishavane	USD $550 + USD $90 for transport − USD $150 for legal costs	Cash, full amount of USD $7,000 not paid
Shurugwi	USD $1,000 (payment in Zimbabwean Dollar, estimation of current value based on the price for three cows)	Cash (17% of respondents reported to have received the full amount on the due date)

The affected households in Mberengwa were supposed to receive comprehensive financial compensation to cover their losses in terms of improvements and disturbances. In Zvishavane, houses were constructed for the relocated community and they were supposed to get financial compensation to cover the replacement of other structures and any other losses they incurred due to disturbances. The community in Shurugwi was given a similar deal but also received agricultural inputs to minimise disruptions as well as financial compensation, which was supposed to cover any other losses and recognised the involuntary nature of the relocation. However, only the community in Shurugwi actually received the full amount and value of financial compensation they were entitled to, although most households had not received payments on the due date.

As provided in section 12(2) of the Communal Land Act, the funds to compensate the affected households in Mberengwa were supposed to come from the Consolidated Revenue Fund and not directly from the local authorities' budget. Documents show that Mberengwa Rural District Council had not received the full amount from central government to effect the payments until July 2002. Thereafter, the cheques stayed for more than 6 months in the District Administrator's office due to 'red tape' before they were handed over to the Chief Executive Officer of the Mberengwa Rural District Council for disbursement to the affected community members. By the time the funds reached the intended beneficiaries, the value had been severely eroded by inflation. What was estimated to be sufficient to replace improvements and compensate disturbances had turned into just enough to buy a 20 kilograms bag of wheat four years later.

In Zvishavane, the affected community sought and obtained a court order which directed the local authority to grant each household USD $7,000, two residential stands in the newly created urban area and a fully constructed four roomed house. Nevertheless, the responsible authorities seem to have defaulted on this judgement and as of September 2018, five years after the relocation, only USD $550 have been paid to each household, of which approximately USD $150 were used to cover the costs of legal representation. Some community members disagreed about the way the payment and the expenses were split amongst them, which contributed to conflicts and rifts within the community.

The lawyer that was hired by the community had negotiated an agreement between the community, the land developer, the Governor of the Midlands Province (Minister of State), and the local authorities. The agreement stipulated that the payment of compensation should be made by the land developer through the Governor's office to the legal representative of the community, who would then transfer the funds to the affected community members. The community feels reliably informed that the agreed amount had been paid in full to the Governor's office and suspects that there have been underhand dealings between the lawyer and other stakeholders. This was supported by the fact that the lawyer contacted the community in 2017 to inform them that their outstanding balances were ready, only to become evasive immediately thereafter and eventually renounce agency without handing over any documentation of the agreement to the community. The community has lost hope of receiving the outstanding amount.

3.4. Rehabilitation of access to public infrastructure, social facilities, communal developments, commons, natural resources, and cultural heritage sites

Physical relocation of communities can have sustained negative effects on the social, economic and cultural development of the affected people, especially if there are no integrated plans or programmes to rehabilitate their livelihoods as well as access to infrastructure, facilities, services, commons, and heritage sites. Whilst there has been a strong policy focus on improving the access of smallholder farmers and rural communities to agricultural land in Zimbabwe, there have been gaps in terms of ensuring access to critical infrastructure, facilities and services in resettlement areas (see CCMT 2014), which particularly affects vulnerable groups, such as children, elderly and people with disabilities or chronic health issues.

The community in Mberengwa, which had occupied communal land before the relocation and was severely restricted in terms of the available land, used to enjoy comprehensive access to social facilities and infrastructure at their previous location. After the relocation, the affected households have gained land but lost direct access to nearly all social facilities, with the exception of a primary school. In order to support the community, two school blocks were constructed by the responsible authorities, a borehole was drilled and two boreholes were repaired in proximity of the new location. The new environment offers better access to water and forests, although half of the respondents reported loss of grazing lands and the community has not received a dip tank they had been promised. In terms of public services, the community has less access to agricultural extension services, which are located far away, and traditional leadership is not as functional as before. The culture of the community has been affected by the lack of a cemetery and sacred places. Community members also reported significant disruption of social relationships due to the relocation, since only part of the community has been resettled to the resettlement area and experienced challenges in integrating in the new community.

Figure 6: Mberengwa - community appraisal of access to public facilities after the relocation (within 15 km)

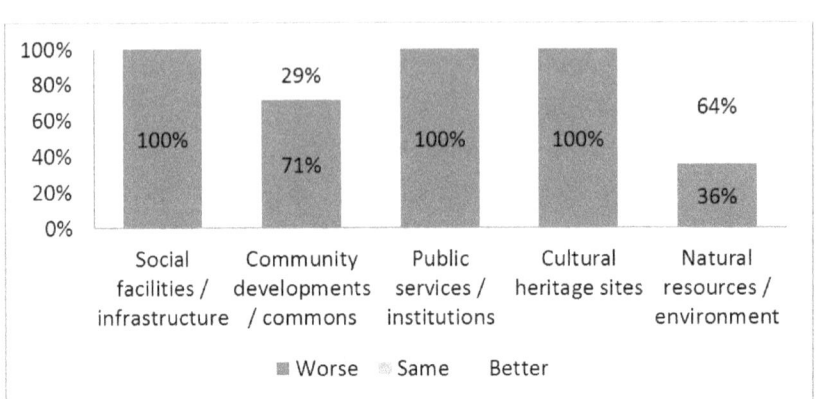

In terms of public infrastructure and social facilities, the community in Zvishavane is in a similar predicament as the one that had been relocated 15 years earlier in Mberengwa. Primary and secondary schools, the clinic and business centre are now 18 kilometres away, while such facilities were located within 5 kilometres distance at the previous settlement. Community members had built a school using their own resources at the former location and they were told by the responsible authorities that this school would be sold to the land developer in order to construct a new school in the area they had been relocated to. The local authorities also promised the construction of a road connecting the community to the business centre, since they are now located within 3 to 4 hours walking distance to public transport. The authorities drilled a borehole, but have not made good on their other promises yet. In contrast to the previous settlement, the community has no access to irrigable land anymore and some community members reported that they had benefited from artisanal mining before the relocation, which is however compensated by the improved agricultural production on the arable land at the new location. They also lost cultural sites and do not have a cemetery anymore, but enjoy similar access to public services as before.

In Zvishavane and Mberengwa, social relationships were negatively affected by restricted access to education. As a result, some households had left their children behind on their own so that they could continue to attend school. Access to ancestral graves was also lost due to the relocation, although 66% of all respondents indicated that they would not have preferred reburials due to their cultural beliefs, even if it would have been offered by the responsible authorities.

Figure 7: Zvishavane - community appraisal of access to public facilities after the relocation (within 15 km)

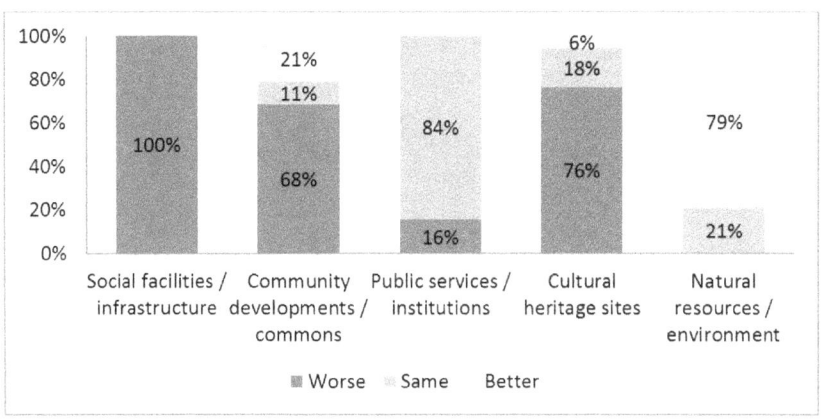

The community in Shurugwi, which had been relocated to pave way for mining, experienced less challenges and changes than the communities in the other two cases. Community members have no access to irrigable land anymore and livelihoods have been negatively affected by the loss of artisanal mining opportunities as well as decreased land size and quality, which also resulted in the loss of shared fields and community projects. However, overall community members reported that they enjoy similar access to public infrastructure, social facilities and community developments as before the relocation. They still have access to health services, a business centre and are connected to a road. Unki mine also constructed a primary and secondary school and drilled boreholes. The community has a cemetery and most public services are as functional as before, although there is less access to sacred forests and veterinary services. However, some community members complained that Unki Mine had not kept the promise to create employment opportunities for community members, especially youths.

Figure 8: Shurugwi - community appraisal of access to public facilities after the relocation (within 15 km)

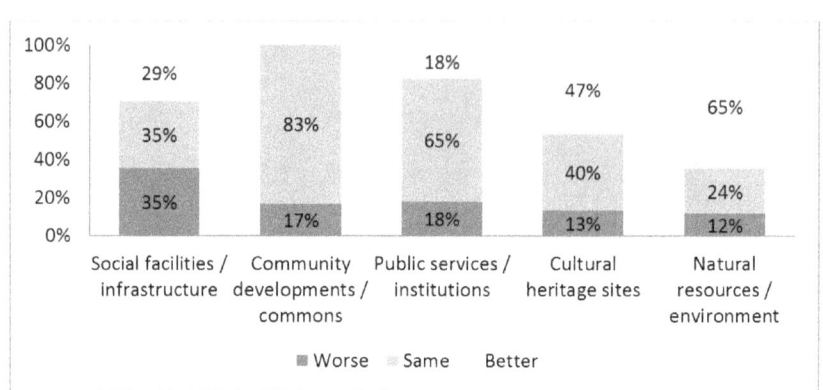

4. Conclusion

4.1. Summary of findings

The affected community in Mberengwa is very dissatisfied with the relocation process and compensation package they received, which basically only consisted of alternative land, transport and assistance with tillage for some of the households. The responsible authorities had not conducted the process in a consultative manner, but comprehensive valuations were carried out. However, the valuations were conducted without the involvement of community members and there was no mutual agreement with the community on compensation. The conflict escalated in demonstrations by community members, who eventually were threatened with eviction. While some felt they were forced to move, others continued to refuse and kept on resisting for the next twenty years, which stalled the growth point development.

After the relocation, the community in Mberengwa was left without housing because compensation was only paid four years later. In the meantime, inflation had nearly completely eradicated the value of the financial compensation which was supposed to provide comprehensive coverage for improvements and disturbance. Although the local authorities supported the rehabilitation of the community by constructing a primary school and drilling boreholes, the affected people had better access to public infrastructure and social facilities prior to the relocation. However, the community has benefited in terms of receiving more adequate land for agriculture. Despite this, it is concerning to note that parts of the community are already facing another possible relocation to pave way for chrome mining activities at their new location, which are already negatively affecting the environment.

The experience of the community in Zvishavane was similar to the one in Mberengwa. In contrast to the community in Mberengwa, people were not left without housing after the relocation, but initially faced severe problems in moving to the new location and clearing and cultivating the land. The houses that had been constructed by the land developer who was involved in the relocation were not equivalent to the buildings the affected people owned before, while the financial compensation they received was not sufficient to cover their losses and make up for the disturbances they endured. In the end, the community was left on their own in terms of rehabilitating their livelihoods. However, since the responsible authorities resettled the community on better land for agriculture, most community members actually managed to improve their livelihoods in the long term. Although this is a positive result, they have no land tenure documents for the allocated land, which renders them vulnerable to further displacements. The community was also negatively affected by losing access to public infrastructure and social facilities, which had a particularly severe impact on vulnerable groups.

Overall, the relocation process in Zvishavane was severely compromised, worsened social relationships and led to severe dissatisfaction and conflicts in the community. The community had not received public notice, was moved within a month of being informed and no valuations were conducted to assess compensation values. In response, the affected community members successfully approached a lawyer and the Administrative Court which ruled in their favour and validated their demand of USD $7,000 compensation per household, two urban stands and replacement of houses. Despite this, the community has not received restitution and there are indications of underhand dealings between involved stakeholders. The case has resulted in the suspension of some officials and is being investigated by a commission of inquiry which was set up in February 2018 to probe into illegal land sales around urban areas since 2005.

The case in Shurugwi presents a very different picture and led to opposite results than the other two cases. The community is the only one reasonably satisfied with the relocation process and compensation package they received. The responsible authorities, which included a mining company, developed public infrastructure and social facilities for the community and provided houses, material support and financial compensation to minimise disruptions and disturbances. It is however important to note that, just as in Zvishavane, the affected people are not satisfied with the replacement of houses because their new houses are said to be smaller and of poorer quality than their previous ones, despite the assessment conducted before the relocation.

Figure 9: Overall level of satisfaction of communities with relocation process and compensation package

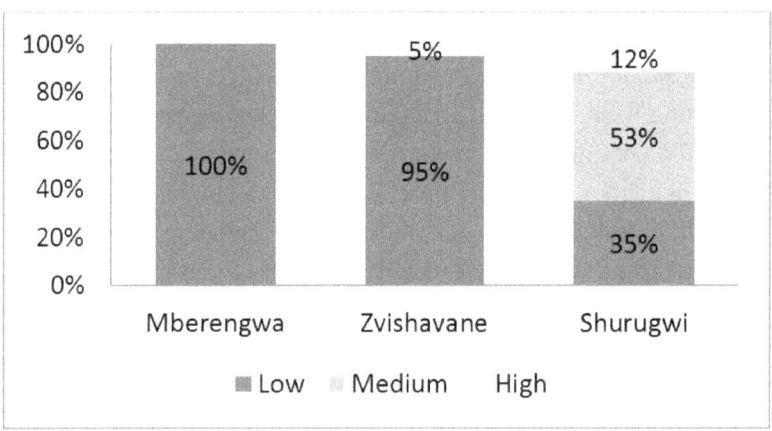

Although no negotiations took place in Shurugwi and the community had no say in the terms and conditions of their relocation and compensation, the affected people received sufficient notice, were publicly consulted by the responsible authorities and also knew about the valuation assessments that were conducted. The affected people decided to not take action against the relocation, although they received some information about their rights by the authorities and reported to have not moved voluntarily. Even though the community received a comprehensive compensation package, which covered most of their losses, they were negatively affected by the relocation in the long term. The households had been relocated on smaller land parcels of poorer quality and as a result the livelihoods of the affected people deteriorated, which raises questions about the sustainability of the assistance that has been provided.

4.2. Recommendations

As the case in Shurugwi shows, public consultations and transparency in advance of displacements are key to increase the acceptability of the process and to avoid the escalation of conflicts and delay of projects. Ideally, the responsible authorities, affected communities or their chosen representatives and relevant third parties engage in fair and balanced negotiations to reach a mutual agreement about the terms and conditions of the relocation and compensation. If such an agreement can be reached, it should be availed to all parties and relevant stakeholders in writing. In order to enable fair and balanced negotiations, the responsible authorities should also inform affected communities about their rights. In a best case scenario, any costs for legal or other representation and related expenses of the community are supposed to be considered and covered by the compensation package.

The communities from Zvishavane and Shurugwi both complained about the size and quality of houses that had been constructed for them, which were not comparable to the ones they previously owned. Compensation should be guided by the principle of equivalence. Any financial compensation, material support or replacement of structures should at least aim at restoring the socio-economic position the affected households were in before the relocation. In order to achieve equivalence, comprehensive valuations and assessments should be carried out at household level to establish compensation values. Conflicts can be avoided, if affected community members are informed about the process and methods of valuations and assessments, and if they have the option to make their own submissions for further consideration. Ideally, the commissioned valuators and assessors are independent parties agreed upon by all stakeholders. The results of neutral assessments accepted by all involved parties can be helpful for negotiations and increase the chances of reaching a mutual agreement.

Although smallholders have a critical role in reviving agricultural production in Zimbabwe and it has been the goal of various government policies to improve their situation, it is concerning that none of the communities in the three cases received specific support in replacing any farming-related improvements on their land, especially with regards to households in Zvishavane and Shurugwi which had access to irrigation facilities before the relocation. The communities in Mberengwa and Zvishavane were also severely affected by disruptions and disturbances of their livelihoods, but have not received adequate compensation and no specific measures were in place to mitigate such risks. Communities should receive adequate support and financial compensation for any disruptions, disturbances or other damages reasonably incurred due to the process of relocation in consideration of the fundamentally involuntary nature of the process. The affected people should also be provided sufficient transport for their movable assets and receive technical assistance or material support in clearing and cultivating new land.

However, the cases in Mberengwa and Zvishavane revealed several challenges with regards to financial compensation. Especially in terms of replacement of structures, financial compensation is not always the most suitable and sustainable method for restoring the previous household situation and it also might not always benefit all household members equally, given gender and other inequalities. In any case, agreements on financial compensation should clearly outline the payment schedule, currency and mode of payment, as well as interest rates applicable to delayed payments. At least partial payment should be done in advance of the relocation in order to enable the communities to prepare for re-establishing their livelihoods at the new location and to avoid a situation like in Mberengwa, where people were left without housing and support systems. The cases in Mberengwa and Zvishavane also showed that it might become complicated for the beneficiaries to actually receive compensation funds, if the funds come from central government or are channelled through the hands of various intermediaries. To avoid any unreasonable delays, local authorities or third parties from the private sector should, whenever feasible, provide compensation to the communities directly and already factor the costs into development plans and budgets at the planning stage of the project.

Agriculture is the key source of livelihoods for most rural communities and the case in Shurugwi points at the negative impact of allocating land which is not at least equivalent in terms of size and quality to the land previously occupied and used by the relocated people. Wherever feasible, alternative land should be arable and of similar size, soil quality, rainfall patterns, trees, and perennial crops. If such land is not available, other types of replacement or compensation should be provided or reasonable measures or programmes agreed upon to provide or enable other sustainable sources of livelihood for the affected people. In addition, adequate actions should be taken to avoid repeated relocations and to improve the security of land tenure of the affected people in order to enable sustainable development. Relocated communities should receive land tenure documents and ideally registration fees should be waived by the authorities as part of the compensation package.

The communities in Mberengwa and Zvishavane lost access to crucial public infrastructure and social facilities due to the relocation, which affected their constitutional socio-economic rights[6], disturbed their social relationships and had a particularly negative impact on vulnerable groups, such as children, elderly and people with disabilities or chronic health issues. The responsible authorities should aim to resettle affected communities in areas with equivalent infrastructure, facilities, services, developments and resources. If this is not feasible, reasonable measures and programmes should be agreed upon to rehabilitate the social, economic and cultural development of the affected communities.

For this purpose, comprehensive impact assessments should be commissioned and conducted at communal level in advance of the relocation. Such impact assessments should weigh risks and opportunities of the relocation in terms of socio-economic development and livelihoods of the affected people, examine access to public infrastructure and services, social facilities, commons and natural resources, as well as propose adequate programmes to mitigate negative impact and to rehabilitate development.[7] Just like valuation assessments, such impact assessments should be carried out in a transparent and participatory manner and inform negotiations of agreements on relocation and compensation.

The case in Shurugwi, which was caused by the Unki platinum project, provides a good example how the involvement of the private sector can positively contribute to the compensation and rehabilitation of relocated communities, while the case in Zvishavane, which involved a land developer, shows that this is far from being guaranteed. Any third party benefiting from the relocation of local communities should reasonably contribute towards the compensation of each household and the rehabilitation of the socio-economic development of the community. In order to avoid situations like in Zvishavane, it is crucial that such contribution is agreed upon and implemented in a transparent and accountable manner.

---

6 Constitution of Zimbabwe Amendment (No. 20) Act, 2013, in particular Section 73-77

7 An example are the comprehensive resettlement regulations in Mozambique which require a "Technical Resettlement Monitoring and Supervision Committee" and socio-economic studies and environmental assessments for preparation of development oriented resettlement plans (CCJP 2014, Annex 6.6)

Key recommendations for relocation and compensation of rural communities

- To give sufficient public notice and conduct public consultations and hearings.
- To inform affected communities about their rights.
- To negotiate the terms and conditions of the relocation with the affected people or their chosen representatives and any relevant third party.
- To reimburse expenses of the affected people for legal or other representation and preparation of any required documentation.
- To make any agreement that has been reached available in written form to all involved parties and relevant stakeholders.
- To commission valuations and assessments of immovable household assets and have them conducted by a neutral party if feasible.
- To inform affected people about the process and methods of the valuation assessment and to provide the option of making own submissions.
- To replace buildings and other improvements based on the principle of equivalence or to provide material support and/or financial compensation that enables equivalent replacement.
- To take reasonable measures for mitigation of disruptions and disturbances.
- To provide technical and material support and/or financial compensation for any disruptions, disturbances or other damages reasonably incurred due to the process.
- To clearly outline the payments schedule, the currency and mode of payment, as well as interest rates applicable to delayed payments in any agreement involving financial compensation.
- To complete replacements of crucial structures and pay at least partial compensation in advance of the relocation.
- To pay or provide compensation directly to the beneficiaries if feasible.
- To factor compensation costs into development plans and budgets at the planning stage of projects.

- To allocate equivalent or better land to the affected people that is at least as suitable for the intended occupation and use as the previously held land.
- To provide, support and enable other sustainable livelihood sources, projects and opportunities, if equivalent alternative land is not available.
- To facilitate registration of land and to waive registration and development fees.
- To commission independent assessments examining the social, economic, cultural, and environmental impact of the displacement in advance of the process.
- To agree upon and take reasonable measures ensuring equivalent or better access to infrastructure, social facilities, public services, and natural resources at the new location.
- To ensure that any third party involved or benefiting from the relocation contributes towards compensation and rehabilitation of the affected people in a transparent and accountable manner.

References

Terminski, B. (2018): "Development-induced Displacement and Resettlement: Theoretical Frameworks and Current Challenges", Thesis, Geneva.

CCJP (2014). "Land Displacement, Involuntary Resettlement and Compensation Practice in the Mining Sector - A Comparative Analysis of Legal and Policy Frameworks in Southern Africa", Catholic Commission for Justice and Peace.

CCMT (2014): "Challenges to Social Service Delivery in Zimbabwe's Resettlement Areas", Centre for Conflict Management and Transformation.

FAO (2008): "Compulsory Acquisition of Land and Compensation", Land Tenure Studies 10, Food and Agriculture Organization of the United Nations.

Gonese, F.T., N. Marongwe, C. Mukora, B. Kinsey (2002). *Land Reform and Resettlement Implementation in Zimbabwe - An Overview of the Programme against Selected International Experiences.* Madison: University of Wisconsin.

Government of Zimbabwe (2014). *Statutory Instrument 53 of 2014, Agricultural Land Settlement (Permit Terms and Conditions) Regulations.* Harare: Government Printer.

—— (2013). *Constitution of Zimbabwe Amendment (No. 20) Act.* Harare: Government Printer.

—— (2006). *Arbitration Act, Chapter 7:15.* Harare: Government Printer.

—— (2002). *Communal Land Act, Chapter 20:04.* Harare: Government Printer.

HRW (2015). "Homeless, Landless, and Destitute - The Plight of Zimbabwe's Tokwe-Mukosi Flood Victims", Human Rights Watch.

IDMC (2008). "The Many Faces of Displacement: IDP's in Zimbabwe", Internal Displacement Monitoring Centre.

Madebwe, C., V. Madebwe, S. Mavusa (2011): "Involuntary Displacement and Resettlement to Make Way for Diamond Mining: the Case of Chiadzwa Villagers in Marange, Zimbabwe", *Journal of Research in Peace, Gender and Development*, 1(10) pp.292-301.

MoLG (2002). "Manual for the Management of Urban Land", Ministry of Local Government, Public Works and National Housing.

SMAIAS (2018). "Locating the Position of Peasants under the "New Dispensation" – A Focus on Land Tenure Issues", Sam Moyo African Institute for Agrarian Studies.

Scoones, I. (2017). "Medium-Scale Farming for Africans – The Native Purchase Areas". Zimbabweland Blog, 6 February 2017.

Thondhlana, G. (2014). "The Local Livelihood Implications of Biofuel Development and Land Acquisitions in Zimbabwe", Africa Initiative and Centre for International Governance Innovation.

Tripathi, S. (2017). "Development, Displacement and Human Rights Violations", *Indian Journal of Public Administration*, 63(4), pp.567-578.

www.ingramcontent.com/pod-product-compliance
Lightning Source LLC
Chambersburg PA
CBHW051613230426
43668CB00013B/2092